ILEX FOUNDATION SERIES 5

JAYA

Also in the Ilex Foundation Series

Dreaming across Boundaries:
The Interpretation of Dreams in Islamic Lands
Edited by L. Marlow

Strī:
Women in Epic Mahābhārata
By Kevin McGrath

Persian Literature and Judeo-Persian Culture:
Collected Writings of Sorour S. Soroudi
Edited by H. E. Chehabi

The Rhetoric of Biography:
Narrating Lives in Persianate Societies
Edited by L. Marlow

The *History* of Beyhaqi
(The History of Sultan Masʿud of Ghazna, 1030–1041)
by Abu'l-Fażl Beyhaq
Translated and with commentary and notes by C. E. Bosworth
Revised and with further commentary by Mohsen Ashtiany

JAYA

PERFORMANCE IN EPIC MAHĀBHĀRATA

Kevin McGRATH

Ilex Foundation
Boston, Massachusetts
and
Center for Hellenic Studies
Trustees for Harvard University
Washington, D. C.

Distributed by Harvard University Press
Cambridge, Massachusetts, and London, England

JAYA: Performance in Epic Mahābhārata
By Kevin McGrath

Kevin McGrath is an associate of the Sanskrit Department at Harvard University. He is the author of *Strī: Women in Epic Mahābhārata* (Ilex Foundation Series 2; 2009) and *The Sanskrit Hero* (2004).

Published by Ilex Foundation, Boston, Massachusetts and the Center for Hellenic Studies, Trustees for Harvard University, Washington, D.C.

Distributed by Harvard University Press, Cambridge, Massachusetts and London, England

Production editor: Christopher Dadian
Cover design: Joni Godlove
Printed in the United States of America

The images on the cover are from a *kīrti-stambha*, or hero stone, in Wagar, the Kacch of Gujarat, c. late eighteenth century. Photo by and courtesy of Leanna McGrath.

Library of Congress Cataloging-in-Publication Data

McGrath, Kevin.
Jaya : performance in epic Mahabharata / Kevin Mcgrath.
p. cm. -- (Ilex foundation series ; 5)
Includes bibliographical references and index.
ISBN 978-0-674-06246-7 (alk. paper)
1. Mahabharata--Criticism, interpretation, etc. I. Title.
BL1138.27.M43 2011
294.5'923047--dc23

2011018111

To G. N., *l'altissimo poéta*

Contents

Acknowledgments

Some of the chapters in this present work began as footnotes or asides in earlier studies, principally *The Sanskrit Hero* and *Strī*. This book continues with ideas touched upon by those earlier works.

I remain constantly indebted to members of the Harvard Mahābhārata Seminar, chaired by Thomas Burke, whose thoughts and words have, for me, amplified the idea of epic performance and its ongoing consequence in the modern subcontinent of India.

I am also profoundly and especially grateful to the following friends and colleagues for their generosity and many kindnesses: Peter Banos, Homi Bhabha, Sugata Bose, Olga Davidson, Maya De, Diana Eck, David Elmer, Robert Goldman, Lilian Handlin, Leonard van der Kuijp, Leanna McGrath, Gregory Nagy, Maurice Pechet, Shashi Tharoor, and Michael Witzel. Douglas Frame was a particularly munificent reader of an early manuscript of the book, and Christopher Dadian has been, as always, an impeccable editor.

If humanism is an intellectual and emotional effort which seeks to understand what we are not, then a comprehension of the nature of metaphor and its composition lies at the heart of that endeavor.

Cambridge, 2011

1

Introduction

THE SPOKEN WORD AND THE WRITTEN WORD are completely different media and only barely correspond, insofar as they represent two differing systems of epistemology. Poetry in its epic condition—during the era before writing—was a widespread medium of value that existed in a state of contingency and performance; and the epic Mahābhārata can be considered an originally incidental text which depicted an idealized heroic Bronze Age culture during such an age of preliteracy. As a work of art the poem sustained a particular social identity in parts of northern India, a function which continues even today. This study examines in detail the generation of a few of the metaphors of that early poem in terms of how the epic presented itself during its own performance.

Composed and improvised upon a foundation of theme and formulaic expression, the Mahābhārata was initially only performed; only later, once a scripted text had become established, did it become an object of recital. This book is an analysis of how the Mahābhārata staged its own performance, or how it expressed itself, and looks principally at the work of one central and arguably archaic poet; the analysis is made evident by a close reading of verses focusing particularly on lines that are spoken by the poet-seer-messenger Saṃjaya Gāvalgaṇi. This poet I consider a firm metaphor of much that concerns the pre-written aspects of the poem and in this kind of inquiry I pursue not simply knowledge but also an understanding of the *nature* of that knowledge.

By epic poetry I signify a *kṣatriya* and Bronze Age literature of an Indo-European provenance. Such society and culture as depicted in this poetry would be preliterate and premonetary.[1] *Kṣatriyas* I define as warriors and their kin-associates, those whose work consists in conflict and rule; the *varṇa* of brahmin is founded upon the operation of solemn ritual and the work of the *vaiṣya* concerns work within a landscape or agriculture. The sacred fire and the oblation, the weapon and bloodshed, and the cultivation of

1. However, in the Droṇa *parvan* the arrows of Arjuna are at one point said to be: *nāmāṅkitāḥ* 'marked with a name' or 'possessing the cipher of a name' (VII.74.7). These are likely to be ideograms, or signs similar to what we know as the "Indus Valley script"; or perhaps they were simply an Arjuna "logo."

earth and its livestock: these are the distinguishing signs of the three social orders or registers which existed in archaic times in northwest India. If we translate the word *kṣatriya* as 'warrior' and consider the epic Mahābhārata as an heroic literature which makes manifest warrior culture, it is possible to identify in the poem certain manners and customs that are distinct aspects of the *varṇa* or 'caste' of warrior life.[2]

This *kṣatriya* quality of epic Mahābhārata is what Jakobson and the Prague School would call "the dominant":

> Verse itself is a system of values; as with any value system, it possesses its own hierarchy of superior and inferior values and one leading value, the dominant, without which ... verse cannot be conceived and evaluated as verse.[3]

Thus by "epic" Mahābhārata, I mean those parts of the poem's cycle which are concerned with warrior culture and values; this is to the exclusion of certain parts of the Poona text which deal with 'law' or *dharma*, with genealogy, or with edifying or brahminical discourse.[4] This "epic" form of the poem as we have it today would constitute what it refers to reflexively as the *Bhārata*; with the addition of *upākhyānas* or 'secondary episodes' this becomes the Great Bhārata, the *Mahābhārata* (I.1.56 and 61).[5] Amartya Sen in his excellent critical scrutiny of the ideas which go to form our understanding of justice writes of *nyāya* and *nīti*, 'realized justice' and 'organizational propriety', respectively.[6] These two dimensions of dharma I would gloss as epic or *kṣatriya* justice, *nyāya*, which is by nature diachronic, and the synchronic view of brahminical *nīti*.[7]

The Bhārata narrative, I would aver, primarily concerns the Pāṇḍavas

2. Hopkins (1888), Watkins (1995), and West (2007) supply the conceptual background for this argument.

3. Jakobson 1987: Chapter 4, 41–42.

4. Hindu jurisprudence often considers the epic as a source for the teaching of how dharma functions in the universe. The "law texts" as revealed in the Śānti *parvan* and the Anuśāsana *parvan* are not the kind of poetry that occurs in any other Indo-European epic and the Mahābhārata is unique in possessing such additions or chapters. However, apart from the *law* itself, what makes any work of art a *classic* is that it embodies the values and codes of valence for a social group who make up the audience of that work of art. A classic is a repository of standard, hence the Mahābhārata today for all of India is *the* classic of social worth. Sukthankar (1944: 12) writes of the Mahābhārata, "it is the most *valuable product* of the entire literature of ancient India" (my emphasis). The poem even portrays the horror of *bheda* 'partition'.

5. At I.53.31, the *sūta* Ugraśravas refers to the *bhāratam mahat* which 'arose from the oceanic mind of the great *ṛṣi*' (*manaḥsāgarasaṃbhūtāṃ maharṣeḥ*; I.53.34).

6. Sen 2009: xv, 20ff.

7. Sen (2009: vii) writes of how it is that our perception of *injustice* allows us to conceive of possible *justice*. This view can be applied with great pertinence to the Mahābhārata: Yudhiṣṭhira's idea of justice is vague and is in fact more a sense of injustice, and Draupadī's view is solely one of revenge for injustice.

and the Kauravas. The matrix of the poem consists in the verses dealing with an opposition between two moieties of a clan based upon the lineages of two half-brothers, whose two lines descend, on the one hand in the patriline, and on the other hand through the matriline. This pattern supplies the fundamental binary structure to the epic.[8]

By "epic" Mahābhārata, I also distinguish the Classical and Sanskrit poem from all the other vernacular and contemporary traditions of the myth which incorporate the visual, the dramatic, the cinematic, and the prosaic tellings of the poem's cycle.[9] Epic poetry in its archetypal foundations is a medium that I consider non-monistic and extensively plural in form; it was and still is by nature inclusive, generative, and divergent. This poetic manner I have discussed in earlier work.[10]

The physical structure of the poem is composed of tens of thousands of repetitive metrical units typically given in the *śloka* meter.[11] The continuous sound of this verse being chanted with varying degrees of emotional expressiveness is made up of primarily descriptive speeches given by the poets, by the dramatis personae themselves, the heroes, and to a much less-

8. From the time of Satyavatī's injunction to her son Vyāsa to impregnate the widows of Vicitravīrya, to Kuntī's supplication of five deities in order to become pregnant, and to Kuntī's niece giving birth to Parikṣit, the descent of lineage in the clan is through the matriline. Bhattacarya (2009) is wrong when he says that I have used this term as a "misnomer." It is during these Pāṇḍava-matriline—as opposed to patriline—generations, that the contention occurs which leads to Kurukṣetra. There are only two possibilities in kinship generation, that of the patriline and that of the matriline; even adoption follows this rule, and to speak of patriliny among the Pāṇḍavas during the time of Vicitravīrya and Pāṇḍu is ridiculous. Even Arjuna, in his marriage to Subhadrā, as she is the niece of Kuntī, is privileging the matriline.

9. Brockington and Brockington (2006), in the introduction to their edited translation of the Rāmāyaṇa, offer a useful and simple overview of how an Indian oral tradition might once have flourished. The great editor and critic Sukthankar (1944: 85ff) dismissed the Vulgate edition of the epic as being thoroughly non-textual in its basis and so inferior, yet I personally do not disdain the Vulgate's place in the overall epic tradition. Sukthankar wrote: "Nīlakaṇṭha's guiding principle [as a critic], on his own admission, was to make the Mahābhārata a *thesaurus of all excellences* (culled no matter from what source); and that text has acquired in modern times an importance out of all proportion to its critical value" (Sukthankar 1944: 85). An editor, just like a poet, draws from a selection of traditions according to certain principles of selection; scholiast and poet actually work similarly within various kinds of textual corpus. The poets and critics who worked within the two primary traditions, the northern and the southern traditions of the epic, sang and athetized for good, well-comprehended, non-random, and not-expedient reasons.

10. McGrath 2004 and 2009. The critical values at work in the Northern and Southern Recensions of the Mahābhārata texts—or what came to be *arranged* as literary texts—have not been examined by scholars. Much as Virgil reformulated the aesthetic values of the Homeric Iliad, and Apollonius of Rhodes reformulated even more broadly various traditions of epic poetry in his Argonautica, so too those early editors or poets made an arrangement of material from which Sukthankar, in a much later century, drew his materials for the Poona text.

11. The *anuṣṭubh*, commonly known as the *śloka*, is made up of two half-verses of sixteen syllables or of four *pādas* of eight syllables.

er extent by dialogues between characters. To hear the Mahābhārata being recited in a temple in India today is to listen to a monody in which various moments receive emphatic flourish accompanied by a gesture of the hand or by embellishments on an accompanying harmonium or even drums. Contemporary recital of the epic—in my experience in Gujarat—is a sung or chanted medium.

In modern India where the epic still flourishes as a vital component of culture and society, the *ṛṣi* or 'ancient sage' Vyāsa is fervently believed to have been an historical figure, who literally dictated the poem to the deity Ganeṣa, who then wrote it down.[12] This is an accepted belief even among learned and distinguished *paṇḍits*: Vyāsa was *the* sole author.[13] Modern Indian culture treats the sign of the epic as an absolute referent and as an object of both belief and *bhakti* or 'worship'.[14]

The mutability of the "text" in modernist India is something which actually delivers vitality and extensiveness to the poem and sustains its importance in current society, which is unlike the Western attitude to such poetry where a rigorous and precise specificity of opus is the result of centuries of work by critics and editors. It is notable that the Mahābhārata as a poetic text—given the enormous efforts that went into sustaining the exactitude of such verbal documents as the Vedas, especially the ṚgVeda—received so little exacting attention and that the poem as it exists now in the twenty-first century is so textually various and diverse and essentially kinetic in its life.[15] The *kṣatriyas* who patronized the song were obviously only interested in the values manifest in the poetry and not in any precision of expression; unlike the Brahmins with their absolute concern for the verbal and tonal preservation of the *mantras* that went to sustain ritual efficacy.

12. The Indian tradition would in fact not consider the Mahābhārata to be "poetry." *Kāvya* is the term used to signify such literature whilst the term *itihāsa* 'history' is used to denote such works as the Mahābhārata, even though it exists in verse form.

13. Das (2009) offers a learned and astute model of how a contemporary Indian intellectual reads the epic. Pattanaik (2008) offers a liberal *hindutva* reading of the Rāmāyaṇa epic. The awful crisis at Ayodhya in 1992 was generated by devotees of the hero Rāma pursuing violent ends at his cult site; the archaic hero still bears great social significance today and the 2010 Allahabad High Court decision only prolongs this crisis.

14. Snodgrass (2006: 21), writing of bards in recent centuries in Rajastan, observes, "Bardless, a family was defenseless in these games of name and status. By singing their patrons' virtues, martial or marital, bardic performers made benefactors appear either as valuable allies or as potentially ruthless enemies. They helped kings secure alliances, negotiate treaties, or avoid war altogether. Leaders, especially those of Tribal origins, also used bards to fashion noble genealogies once they ascended to power. And bardic genealogies, histories, and poems of praise were recited long after their initial composition, thus influencing the way later generations of Rajasthanis understood their state's past."

15. Hiltebeitel (2000), Mankekar (1999), and Sax (2002) are notable scholars in this field of how the vernacular aspects of the epic are active in contemporary Indian culture.

Until the 1940s there was no critical tradition—in a Western sense—that "fixed" the certainty of the text.

Central to the thought of this book is the idea of a song called *Jaya*, the original poem about a conflict between two fraternal sides of a clan that concludes in a great and absolutely destructive battle.[16] This is the proto-song of the *ṛṣi* Vyāsa, referred to at I.56.19.[17] This he teaches to his son Śuka and then to others among his disciples and peers (I.1.63); among those it was Nārada who 'declared it to the deities' (*nārado'śrāvayad devān;* I.1.64).[18] Only when all the Pāṇḍavas were deceased, that is after the narrative which is detailed in the epic as we now have it had ended, only then when Yudhiṣṭhira and family were dead, did Vyāsa *abravīt bhāratam̟ loke mānuṣe* 'he spoke the Bhārata in the human world' (I.1.56). What constituted Jaya, this song that in its repetitions generated the poetry which we now know as the Mahābhārata, is impossible to re-form; it remains only as the original signifier of the poem and first sign of the epic's performance. Yet it is this signifier which has effected all other subsequent works which come under that first rubric, that initial ordering of poetic valence and worth which ultimately made for the total composition. As such, Jaya is arguably the sacred and impersonal force which underlies *all* tellings of the Mahābhārata and is the source of all efficacy in performance of the epic, insofar as it is *the* seminal and irretrievable spring of words for the poem.[19]

For the purposes of this study I focus particularly on three poets who, in different ways and at different moments in the early history of the song, speak the words of the epic. They are Vyāsa, Vaiśaṃpāyana, and Saṃjaya. It is the contention of this book that of all the poets in the Mahābhārata it is actually Saṃjaya who is the one closest to those first tellings of the epic, not Vyāsa. Certainly, Vyāsa is *reputed* to be the originator and source of the work, but that remains conceptual and hypothetical and is really unattested;

16. From the verbal root √*ji, jayati* 'he conquers'. Mani, in his Encyclopaedia, under the lemma Jaya, states the contemporary Indian view on how the poem developed: "They say that the Bhārata written by Vyāsa consisted only of eight thousand and eight hundred stanzas. To these ... Vaiśaṃpāyana added fifteen thousand, two hundred stanzas and this great book was given the name Bhārata ... When Sūta recited this book to other hermits in Naimiśāraṇya the book had a lakh of stanzas. Henceforward the book was called Mahābhārata."

17. Throughout the course of this book I employ the word "song" in the sense that it is used by Lord in *The Singer of Tales* (1960), or M. C. Smith, *India's Sacred Song* (1992), or Nagy, *Poetry As Performance* (1996a). A song is something that is primarily acoustic; writing or a script is primarily silent.

18. At XVIII.5.46, the telling of the poem by father to son is reiterated.

19. Fitzgerald (2006: 272ff) has an alternative and well-argued hypothesis concerning what he terms the "main *MBh*." by which he explains how the poem came to be what it is now. Hiltebeitel (2006: 229) discusses the situation in terms of what he calls "braided frames."

he is in fact neutral, supplying the absolute form of the poem only in reference, something that is not to be actually apprehended in words by an ascertaining humanity. In the context of the poem as we now have it today, it is the *sūta* Saṃjaya, the singer who—in terms of his senses—is nearest to the events which are described in the central drama of the narrative.

From a strictly diachronic point of view, Vyāsa—even though he is actually inhuman and supernatural—is of an earlier generation, being the one who sires Pāṇḍu and Dhṛtarāṣṭra. Saṃjaya is of an intermediate generation, being somewhat of the age of the heroes themselves. Vaiśaṃpāyana is active in an age that is three generations later and much removed in time from all the events in the poem; his voice is thoroughly retrojective.

As we shall see in the next chapter, Saṃjaya is arguably nearer to the preliterate world of orally composed poetry, whilst Vaiśaṃpāyana—the poet-assistant or disciple of Vyāsa—is more a voice of the literate world. The latter is not *active* in the drama of the poem and merely receives a transmission of poetry from Vyāsa and relates this *material*, whereas Saṃjaya receives a transmission of poetic *skill* from the venerable sage or master. One is substantial the other is formal: Saṃjaya is closer to the absolute pattern of Vyāsa's idea of the epic, whereas Vaiśaṃpāyana only supplies a simulacrum of what he has sensibly received.[20] On a more political level, Saṃjaya is, as we shall see, closely involved with the life of the Kaurava king, Dhṛtaraṣṭra, whilst Vaiśaṃpāyana—as the poet to King Janemejaya, who is the great-grandson of Arjuna—is closely engaged with the Pāṇḍava side of the clan.

In my book *The Sanskrit Hero* I argued that Karṇa was ostensibly the closest to the pattern or paradigm of how a hero was generally *typed* in Indo-European literature.[21] It is significant that one of the most common epithets which Karṇa receives in the course of the Mahābhārata is *sūtaputra* 'son of a *sūta* or poet'; the term *sūta* is also one that Saṃjaya frequently receives.[22] It is difficult and sometimes contentious to speak of what is *older* in the epic, but there is something about both Karṇa and Saṃjaya that is *primary* to the form of this poem, an idea that I develop in Chapter Two.

There are two fundamental assumptions underlying the whole of this work. Firstly, I adhere to the model of epic multiform preliteracy as developed by Gregory Nagy; I amplify a specific component of this view in Chapter Two.[23]

20. Certainly the poetry of the ṚgVeda was composed and sustained by a preliterate tradition. Yet because of its ritual and sacerdotal purpose the exactitude of its performance and transmission was absolutely and irrefragably fixed at an early point in time. One cannot compare such a process with that of epic Mahābhārata.

21. McGrath 2004.

22. As for example at V.46.12.

23. Nagy 1996a.

Secondly, I am in full accord with the nature of Indo-European culture, society, and poetics, an idea developed by Watkins and recently re-examined by West.[24] I examined these IE aspects of Mahābhārata at length in *The Sanskrit Hero*.[25] I also assume the existence of a broad and rich terrain made up of visual and audial accounts concerning heroic lives which surround and encompass the actual *mythopoeia* of the epic.[26] It is this terrain which makes for the vitality and dynamism of the epic Mahābhārata in the subcontinent today.

This book is in the tradition of *Quellenforschung*, a research into the stylistic sources of the present poem and examination of the composition rather than the reception of the work; this is my intellectual *bias*. One speaks about The Epic, but there are various and constantly varying manifestations of this polytropic literary phenomenon: there are sources for the poem, there is the poem itself existing within a synchronic merging of traditions and performative interpretation, and then there are the many and various audiences which continue into the twenty-first century, both within India and without.[27]

In what I would describe as an *epic event* one can conceptually distinguish the song, the performance or performer, and the critically-minded editors of the epic poetry. Originally, in the ancient hypothetical Bronze Age days of composition-in-performance, the first two of these categories were merged and indistinct, for epic song was created or arranged during its performance. In later centuries, as I show in the next chapter, song and performance became distinctly separate entities or events. Thereafter, once writing became socially established as a means of literary record there arose the need for critically trained editors who worked according to set principles of literary value: values that concerned beauty of metaphor, standards of formal composition and diction, as well as and perhaps most importantly—for India—notions of spiritual or dogmatic belief.

In the following chapter I examine the nature of poetic inspiration from the two points of view of Saṃjaya and of Vaiśaṃpāyana. The third chapter analyzes the character and authority of Saṃjaya as a distinct personage as he is depicted in the early stages of the epic. Chapter Four is the principal core

24. Watkins 1995; West 2007.

25. McGrath 2004, and to a lesser extent in McGrath 2009.

26. Burgess (2009) and Snodgrass (1998) offer good paradigms for the methodology of this kind of thinking.

27. Similarly, when William Shakespeare in his cycle of history plays portrayed an idealized lineage of the House of Tudor through time, he drew upon the works of Holinshead and others and merged that material into a series of thematically singular and unitary dramas. These continue to be interpreted and performed today even outside of Britain and in many various media; also, songs and speeches from these dramas often maintain their own and separate lives.

of this book and deals with the battle books and *how* it is that the poet sings of the events at Kurukṣetra: these four books—Six to Nine—are the central and generative event of the epic poem and it is here that *Jaya* or 'victory' is actually at stake and operating as the focal signifier. Chapter Four demonstrates in substance what has been argued as a pattern in Chapter Two. Chapter Four also offers a brief overview of how Saṃjaya exemplifies his extraordinary creativity and inventiveness in embellishing a world of violence, destruction, and death, with imagery that is aesthetically pleasing: death is translated into another language of lovely and fertile scenery via similes and metaphors of great beauty. Chapter Five examines the structural counterpoint that occurs within the poem between the poet Saṃjaya and the hero Duryodhana, taking Books Ten and Eleven as text.

My critical methods are thoroughly inductive and inferential and eschew any a priori thinking: I work with grammar, syntax, and lexicon and read slowly. I have used the Critical Edition of the Mahābhārata as established by the Bhandharkar Oriental Institute under the original supervision of Sukthankar.[28] Occasionally I have turned to the so-called Vulgate text where the invaluable scholia of the *paṇḍit* Nīlakaṇṭha has been appended.[29] In order to perform essential word searches of the text I have used the online version of the poem made available by J. D. Smith. The wonderful *Index of Names* compiled by Sörensen is always a useful and vital instrument for any Mahābhārata research.

To quote from the great Sukthankar, "the renown of the Bhāratavarṣa ... is for all time inseparably linked with the Mahābhārata, which is, in more senses than one the greatest epic the world has produced ... a work which is in a unique manner bound up with the history of the Indian people and the prestige of Indian scholarship."[30]

28. The BORI Poona (nowadays Pune) version critically combines manuscripts of both the Northern Recension and the Southern Recension traditions; the latter is usually referred to as the *textus ornatior* and is compiled in twenty-four rather than eighteen books. Sukthankar wrote about the Southern Version, saying that it "impresses us thus by its *precision, schematization, and thoroughly practical outlook.*" He added, "Compared with it, the Northern Recension is distinctly vague, unsystematic, sometimes even inconsequent, *more like a story rather naively narrated*" (Sukthankar 1944: 48).

29. What is known as the Bhāratabhāvadīpa 'lamp of truth for the Bhārata'.

30. Sukthankar 1944: 9. Shashi Tharoor in his 1989 novel—which is founded upon Mahābhārata narrative and characters and depicts events during the 1940s in India—would go so far as to say that the poem is the "charter myth" of modern Indian society, the epitome of its history and temporal extent, or the mythical *res gestae* of the present Republic (personal communication). Just as Greece is called, by Greeks, Hellas, so India today is referred to, by Indians, as Bhārat; thus the Great Bhārata and the place Bhārat, simply on a nominal level are intimately connected. The eponymous man Bharata was the child of Śakuntalā and Duṣyanta, a proto-mythical 'imperial ruler' (*cakravartin*) of northern India.

2

Sound and Vision

THERE ARE FOUR POETS who perform the epic Mahābhārata, five if one includes the nameless and invisible voice of the poet who impersonally pronounces the work, the unidentified but implicit master-narrator.[1] This makes for an unusual system of dimensions for the poem as frames of reference open and close and various distinct perspectives shift about one point, that of the central and intrinsic narrative. I would like to examine these levels of poetic configuration in the light of Nagy's distinction between the *aoidós* and the *rhapsōidós* and develop certain aspects of the model given in the second chapter of his book, *Homeric Questions*.[2] I shall delineate the system of poetic voices at work in the epic, and in Chapter Four expand this structural model in order to demonstrate how the system substantially operates.

Briefly, there is the arch-poet Vyāsa, who is reputed to have made the complete poem. He is said to have instructed Vaiśaṃpāyana, a bard who had received the poem audially from Vyāsa and thereafter recited that work.[3] This recitation occurs at the snake sacrifice of King Janamejaya, the final king-patron of the poem and son of Parīkṣit, the grandson of Arjuna. In the third place is Ugraśravas, who had heard the recital of Vaiśaṃpāyana, and who begins the epic as we have it today.[4]

Central to the present eighteen books of the poem are Books Six to Nine, which describe events and speeches during the great and final battle at Kurukṣetra. This part of the poem is sung by a fourth poet, Saṃjaya, the *sūta* or 'bard', a class of poet who traditionally also drove the royal chariot; he addresses the old and blind king, Dhṛtarāṣṭra. Exchanges between these

1. An earlier version of this chapter was submitted to the *Journal of the Royal Asiatic Society*. In his contribution to *Epic Undertakings* (R. Goldman and M. Tokunaga, eds., Motilal Banarsidass, 2009: 41n28), Simon Brodbeck, a reader for *JRAS*, acknowledged an article submitted to the journal by an author "unknown to [him]" and gave a limited summary of points in that article that supported his present argument. Since the publication of *Epic Undertakings* Mr Brodbeck has confirmed that the work was mine (personal correspondence).

2. Nagy 1996a; see also1996b and 2003.

3. He is what would be called a *pāṭhaka*, a 'reciter', in more pre-modern terms.

4. The Snake Sacrifice, intrinsic to the first half of the Ādi *parvan*, is performed by Janamejaya in revenge for the death of his father, Parīkṣit, caused by the bite of a snake.

two figures also occur throughout the course of the entire epic as the text shifts between its various planes of poetic authority. The battle books are the poetic domain of Saṃjaya.[5]

There exists no neat and simple framing or transition however, whereby one box opens onto another box or vice versa: this does not happen. For instance, the voice of Saṃjaya is heard throughout the course of the poem—not often but occasionally—and not simply during the four battle books but everywhere. Similarly, the voice of the magus-poet Vyāsa appears and disappears throughout the course of the telling, where he speaks—usually within the language of Vaiśaṃpāyana—as an actual character inside the story and affects the emotional state of other characters; it is as if the Homeric poet were to take part in the narrative of the Iliad and interact with the heroes in the poem.[6] The voice of Saṃjaya is also sung by Ugraśravas, long before Vaiśaṃpāyana appears, in the Ādi *parvan*; and Vaiśaṃpāyana appears—albeit briefly and almost nominally—during the four battle books. The mutual imbrication of these four poetic voices thus makes for great and sometimes impenetrable narrative complexity.

Hence the idea of framing or boxing is actually more a question of *voicing*: who is imitating whom at any one point? Essentially, Vaiśaṃpāyana dramatizes the voice of Vyāsa and Saṃjaya; only the words of Ugraśravas are given directly by himself, and he sings the speeches of Vaiśaṃpāyana. There is an hypothetical speaker of the epic who exists without title and who must—existentially—be singing the words of Ugraśravas: just as an hypothetical Homer sings Iliad. Thus our basic model of three or four poets or framing voices—excluding the outer hypothetical voice—is thoroughly loaded with exception, yet the principle of separate creative personae at work holds firm.

Mahābhārata, in its origins, was a 'warrior' or *kṣatriya* literature, a poetry performed—except in the case of Ugraśravas who virtually does not figure in the poem—before kings. It dramatized the crises and dilemmas that Yudhiṣṭhira, the focal ruler of the epic, confronted during his life in order to secure his kingdom. The poem as it exists now was putatively put into writing at some time in the early centuries of the Common Era by a brahmin or priestly clan, the Bhārgavas, descended from the *ṛṣi* or 'seer' Bhṛgu.[7] This scripted text must have been anterior to what we now know as the

5. Except for when there is an obvious interpolation concerning *Vaiṣṇava* myth, as at IX.34–55.

6. To draw a term from Sanskrit drama, Vyāsa behaves as if he were the *sūtradhāra*, the 'manager' of the narrative or stage. He keeps the "thread" of the story moving, maintaining its progress.

7. Sukthankar 1944: 278ff.

Northern and Southern Recensions and it was this early redaction—favoring a Vaiṣṇava view of the cosmos—that brought Vyāsa to the fore as the central poet-composer of the work.[8]

Vyāsa appears and disappears within the narrative itself and influences the course of the drama by announcing how the future is to appear. He was also the poet who, as biological father, generated the two rival clans of the epic as *the* male ancestor of the principal heroic characters.[9] In terms of poetry, it is his mind that is ideally co-extensive with the whole epic and his place in the work is profoundly synchronic in nature; he is the ultimate archetype of the poem, so the poem states. Vaiśaṃpāyana maintains a more diachronic presence throughout the poem.

Much has been written over the years as to the nature of how "earlier" and "later" components of the epic Mahābhārata were constituted.[10] I would like to propose an alternative aetiology in which I employ a model developed by Gregory Nagy in his analyses of Greek epic poetry. In this model Nagy distinguishes between the *aoidós* and the *rhapsōidós*, two distinct kinds of speaker.

The *aoidós* composes his verse during performance, whereas the *rhapsōidós* recites from memory what he has previously heard from other poets. For the *rhapsōidós,* the words of the poem would be a script *for* or *of* an event; for the *aoidós*, the script is merely ideal and unspoken, for it is the TRADITION itself that is responding to any given social context.[11] Formally, the words of the *rhapsōidós* presuppose the prior existence of the *aoidós*, as creatively—at some point—the latter must precede the former in time.

To repeat, there exist three levels of verse composition in Mahābhārata—if we exclude an hypothetical first singing of the epic by Vyāsa—which are proclaimed by Ugraśravas, by Vaiśaṃpāyana, and thirdly by the *sūta* Saṃjaya.[12] Applying the Nagy evolutionary model for an epic poetics we ar-

8. By *vaiṣṇava* I understand the sectarian devotion given to the deity Viṣṇu, rather than to the deities Śiva or Devī or to others. Kṛṣṇa can be considered as an aspect of Viṣṇu.

9. Even though Mahābhārata is an Indo-European epic that is closely cognate with the Iliad, in its massive variety and extent it is unlike the unified and closely involved Homeric corpus. Unlike the Greek epics, the Sanskrit epic—as we noted in Chapter One—continues to flourish as a vital and thoroughly vibrant component of modern Indian—and not only Hindu—society. This cannot be stressed enough: the text is *not* frozen but continues to live and develop in time and is indeed expanding.

10. This is akin to the "Homeric Question." Cf. J. D. Smith 1987: 591–611; M. C. Smith 1992; and Brockington and Schreiner 1999.

11. Nagy 2003: 2; 1996b: Ch.2 *passim*.

12. I give the diachronic and historical order of composition here in the poem as we now have it: Ugraśravas opens the work, and Vaiṣaṃpāyana only enters later, followed by Saṃjaya. These poetic frames are in fact constantly shifting throughout the course of the work as the narrative voice moves among these poets and the perspective alters, supplying the epic with a

rive at a possible scheme for Mahābhārata development. Allow me to make three organizational comments on this *system* of poetry:

Firstly, Vaiśaṃpāyana does not make his actual entry into the poem until the fifty-fourth *adhyāya*, where he is instructed by Vyāsa (I.54.22):

> tad asmai sarvam ācakṣva yan mattaḥ śrutavān asi
>
> Tell all that to him, which you have heard from me.[13]

Vaiśaṃpāyana subsequently announces—and this marks his point of entry into the poem—that, *pravakṣyāmi mataṃ kṛtsnaṃ vyāsasya* 'I shall pronounce the entire thought of Vyāsa' (I.55.2).[14] There is no indication as to where or when this original performance—or several performances—took place: it remains like the master signifier to the narrative, implying all other performances, and yet is without active presentation itself. It is that primary source of value, that primary sign which generates all other signs yet which does not actually—within the compass of the epic—phenomenally exist. Vaiśaṃpāyana's version is described as being *adhītaṃ purā samyag* 'once learned entirely' (I.5.4). It is this recitation of Vaiśaṃpāyana's that Ugraśravas learned from his own father.[15]

At the snake sacrifice, it was Janamejaya who asked Vyāsa to sing the poem and the *ṛṣi* requests that his disciple Vaiśaṃpāyana perform this song of the *carita*: the 'narrative' of the two factions in the family and of the *bheda*, the 'break' that occurred between them (I.54.18–19; and 23–24).[16] Hereafter, this is what Ugraśravas recounts, or is recounting, staging the exchanges between Janamejaya and Vaiśaṃpāyana; it is Vaiśaṃpāyana who, in turn, stages the exchanges between Dhṛtarāṣṭra and Saṃjaya.[17]

Ugraśravas himself had declared earlier that *śrutvā ham* 'I heard' the epic recitation from Vaiśaṃpāyana (I.1.10), which had been originally *dvaipāyena ... proktam* 'declared by Vyāsa' before the deities and *brahmarṣis*

---

fabric of great structural and inwoven complication. Presumably this authorial feat occurred during the Bhārgava recension. There exist small exceptions to this order.

13. *All that* concerns 'the schism of Kurus and Pāṇḍavas' (*kurūṇāṃ pāṇḍavānām ... bhedo;* I.54.22). *Bheda* can also be construed as 'partition'. "Him" denotes King Janamejaya, the patron of this performance which is being commanded. Hiltebeitel (2006: 246), makes the significant observation that after XII.335.8: "this is the only time in the entire epic where Vyāsa, seated as an otherwise silent though not entirely inactive attendee at Janamejaya's snake sacrifice, gives Janamejaya a solely verbal reply."

14. This formula is repeated at I.56.12.

15. *Yad adhītaṃ ca pitrā me samyak caiva tato mayā* (I.5.5).

16. At this point in the poem, Vaiśaṃpāyana depicts three components to the epic: the *bheda*, the 'break' that ensues from the improper gambling, the time spent in the forest by the Pāṇḍavas, and the great battle of Kurukṣetra (I.55.5).

17. As I have stated, there are exceptions to this narrative structure, as when Saṃjaya in Book One is speaking long before Vaiśaṃpāyana has even entered the poem.

'divine seers' (I.1.15).[18] Vaiśaṃpāyana had 'by the command of Vyāsa' (*dvaipāyanājñā*), then repeated this song before king Janamejaya (I.1.18).[19] This is actually what Ugraśravas later recites: *nigadāmi*, he says, 'I proclaim' (I.56). Ugraśravas rehearses what he has heard Vaiśaṃpāyana declaim, for he never heard the actual song of Vyāsa.[20] It is a moot question as to why the ascetics in the forest, the brahmin *munis*, wish to hear this Bhārata however, this heroic song of Jaya.

In a nutshell, the nuclear pattern of poetic transmission within the epic—according to its own self-representation—is: Vyāsa > Vaiśaṃpāyana > Ugraśravas. This is made opaquely complex however, for Saṃjaya is not simply a poet within Vyāsa's song but an actual character in the poem, and similarly, Vyāsa himself also appears as a character. This ambiguity and ambivalence essentially makes the poem irrationally complicated. Again, the fact that Vyāsa supplied and informed the mind and intellect of Saṃjaya with the inspirational skills to sing the battle books arguably places Saṃjaya closer to the hypothetical first-singing of the poem, which Vyāsa then resings. Saṃjaya, in that reading, would himself become the maestro of the epic.[21]

This is an illogical box of mirrors: such is the beautiful and subtle refraction of the poets and editors who over many centuries of time have unbreakably composed the epic. At best one can delineate and discern certain skeletal systems or economies of poetry, yet the song itself will always remain—because of these sophisticated internal tensions and replications—irrefragable and irreducible.[22] The effort of an analyst in this sense can only ever attempt the merely heuristic; for what often seems to be inconcinnity within the formation of poetry is actually a highly refined synthesis of dramatic means.

The poem is thus intricately, if not elusively, folded and refolded upon itself with great and inscrutable artistry: there is no simple beginning and no

18. I sometimes maintain the convention for those who are unfamiliar with the epic, of supplying proper names in the place of epithets, kennings, patronyms, or metronyms. Dvaipāyana 'island born', signifies the islet in the Gaṅgā where Vyāsa received his nativity.

19. 'The great seer spoke the Bhārata in this human world' (*abravīt bhāratam loke mānuṣe'smin mahārṣiḥ;* I.1.56). The audience also learns that, before this actually occurred he had already 'instructed' (*adhyāpayat*), his son Śuka as well as other great seers in the Bhārata (I.1.63).

20. It is unclear whether Ugraśravas heard the song from Vaiśaṃpāyaṇa or from his own father, who had heard the other poet's recitation.

21. That model would be: Saṃjaya > Vyāsa > Vaiśaṃpāyana > Ugraśravas. This schema is developed further in Chapter Four, below.

22. Arguably, one could aver that *myth* is never reasonable, for that is its nature.

simple transition between frames, speakers, or poets. What now exists in the Poona text is the constant mirroring and enactment of speeches given in three voices and all contained in the one untitled and summary speech. What is clearly identifiable as one sole and integral voice, however, is the song of Saṃjaya in the four battle books; for there, the poet recounts to his patron-king the deeds of the battlefield. Vaiśaṃpāyana does make an appearance in these four books but only in response to a brief query by his patron, Janamejaya, to tell what Saṃjaya said next; this is an inconsequential and dramatic overture-device that in no way affects the tempo, substance, or form of the narrative and these infrequent lines that mention his cursory entries and exits could easily be elided without any effect.

There is no clear, single series of transmission of form within the epic, for within the narrative the revealing of these transactions goes back and forth, *not* in simple diachrony but in a complex and non-linear pattern. To make this paradigm more compound and multifarious Vyāsa and Saṃjaya speak not just as poets but also as characters engaged in the dialogue itself. Curiously, Vyāsa's version of the Bhārata poem is said to have contained an hundred *parvans*.[23] Later, when Ugraśravas repeats this song, the epic has been re-organized into eighteen 'books' or *parvans*, the arrangement which we now possess (I.2.70–71).[24]

Everything that Saṃjaya formally declaims—the four central battle books—he "sees," and his report to his king-patron is by virtue of divine eyesight granted to him by Vyāsa: he sees *manasā* 'with his mind'. This ability of *divyadarśitvam* 'divine vision' forsakes him at X.9.58, when, at the death of Duryodhana he is overwhelmed by grief.[25] Vyāsa, who possesses the vision to be able to perceive "everything" in an absolute sense, granted Saṃjaya this inspiration (V.2.11):

> prakāśaṃ vā rahasyaṃ vā rātrau vā yadi vā divā
> manasā cintitam api sarvaṃ vetsyati saṃjayaḥ
>
> Apparent or not apparent, by day or if at night,
> Saṃjaya will observe all, even what is thought by mind.

Later in the poem the audience hears that Kṛṣṇa has also provided the poet with an exceptional visionary ability: *prādāt ... divyaṃ cakṣur* 'he gave divine

23. The *anukramaṇī* or 'list of contents' is organized around an hundred titles: these are what we know nowadays as sub-*parvans*, existing within the canonical eighteen major *parvans* (I.2.34ff).

24. Incidentally, from the opening of the Bhīṣma *parvan* to the end of the Strī *parvan* there are twelve sub-*parvans*.

25. As we shall see, Saṃjaya later tells the old king that he was actually a participant in the battle (VII.70.41). This functions both as a magnification and a dramatic realization of Saṃjaya's powers of imagination. Extending this range of experience, Vyāsa later saves his "substitute" from being killed by Dhṛṣṭadyumna at IX.28.37. See below, Chapter Four.

vision' to Saṃjaya (V.129.13).[26] It is this distinct visual capacity that enables him to witness the theophany of Kṛṣṇa, the *ghoram ātmānaṃ keśavasya* 'the terrific self of Keśava', whilst all the others present in the *sabhā* are overwhelmed and close their eyes.

Vyāsa's comprehension of the epic world as it is represented in poetry is entire, there is no further reference beyond his consciousness: he is *pratyakṣadarśī ... bhūtabhavyabhaviṣyavit* 'one who has before his eyes the past, present and the future' (VI.2.2).[27] Vyāsa is not actually a human being but an ancient Vedic-style *ṛṣi*, one who comes and goes at will throughout the poem, participating in the dialogues as he speaks about the future and the past; he also possesses both divine foresight and hindsight.[28] To make an analogy, Vyāsa is virtually in the place of the Hesiodic Muses, who know the past, the present, and what is to be and how to make the untrue appear true.[29] Yet he appears within the composition himself, modifying both the words and the action of the narrative, and so eluding analysis like an *ur*-signifier.

Considering this hypothetical and assumed song which Vaiśaṃpāyana gives voice to when he enacts the epic that he heard Vyāsa originally perform, we face the question as to where *exactly* is the song of Saṃjaya uttered, where does it *actually* fit? Is it really implicit in the undisclosed micro-epic of Vyāsa, being a technical and dramatic device of the *ṛṣi*? Or, is it something that Vaiśaṃpāyana gives presence to in his performance because he is supplying rhetorical force to the core vehicle of the narrative, that is, to the great battle itself? Such a question must again remain simply heuristic and without answer.

Nevertheless, the inspirational capacity of Saṃjaya—as the poet in a conceptual and motive fashion—supplies an essential component to any understanding of heroic poetics. What appears before Saṃjaya's eyes is the *myth*, he actually "sees" the heroes on the battlefield, unlike the two other poets in the song who have "heard" their vision from prior poets.[30]

26. It is said that Droṇa, Bhīṣma, and Vidura received a similar momentary benefit from the hero-deity. This is unlike the sacred inspirational and sustained technique that Saṃjaya received from maestro Vyāsa however. Vyāsa transmits this gift to no one else in the poem.

27. This portrayal re-occurs at VI.14.1.

28. His name implies this: from *vy-2√as* 'to arrange, dispose'. As he is the generator of both epic lineage and epic text, the Mahābhārata is, in prototype, *his* song about *his* own biological descendants: the five generations from Paṇḍu to Janamejaya; six, if one includes Vyāsa himself. The span of those years is compressed during the singing of the Mahābhārata into one continuous event where frame meets seamlessly with frame.

29. Theogony 26–32. As master of truth he dominates the speech act.

30. Principally Ugraśravas and Vaiśaṃpāyana. Vyāsa too, one must assume, "sees" his poem, although he is more like the Memory who contains or knows a complete repertoire of the work: he *is* the absolute source and mental imprint of the poetry. It is worth noting

His speech is actually that of the heroes, directly, without mediation, the ipsissima verba. The old king, requesting that Saṃjaya tell him of how something transpired, often says to him *tattvena kuśalo hy asi* 'for you are one conversant with TRUTH' (VII.106.16).[31] His words relate experience of events, whereas the words of Vaiśaṃpāyana only tell of words that have been heard from another poet.

That knowledge is visual, it is not something that Saṃjaya has heard. In modification of this model, however, earlier on in the same *parvan* when the old king is inquiring about what happened to Droṇa, Saṃjaya admits to being a poet who is *pratyakṣadarśivān* 'one who has seen what is before his eyes'. Then he immediately proceeds to tell of what Droṇa "said"! (VII.11.1).

Let us briefly recapitulate the compositional structure of Mahābhārata so far. The original song in toto is ostensibly sung by Vyāsa: this is how the poem represents itself although Vyāsa is never actually heard to declaim that *ur*-song but only appears as one of the supernatural characters in the poem; that song is simply an abstract reference in the poem or its *hypostasis*. Most of the epic is performed by Vaiśaṃpāyana, one of whose dramatis personae is Saṃjaya, who himself performs the core battle scenes of the poem, in quotes, as it were, and who incidentally appears elsewhere speaking to the heroes in person, particularly in the Udyoga *parvan*. The figure of the *sūta* Ugraśravas is really only a containing or framing vehicle for all that Vaiśaṃpāyana speaks, the outer skin or envelope of the work, essentially its beginning and end.

It is entirely fitting that the commencement of the poem begins with a poet whose name indicates that he possesses 'terrific fame' (*ugraśravas*). Epic, as we know it is a conductor or medium of heroic 'fame' (*kīrti*), being what a hero exchanges his life for: that is the value of life for a *kṣatriya*.[32]

In sum, concerning the poetic composition of Mahāhābharata, Vyāsa and Saṃjaya are visually or experientially inspired; Vaiśaṃpāyana and Ugraśravas are merely audially inspired, their epic knowledge comes "secondhand."[33] The poetry of Saṃjaya is spontaneously created, whereas

---

that the central body of the poem—the battle books, the "core" of the epic—are related by a Kaurava poet, *not* by a Pāṇḍava *sūta*, albeit one critical of Dhṛtarāṣṭra's lack of policy. Saṃjaya also participates in the battle itself, such is the degree of his engagement with the events of the poem.

31. 'Exactly as it happened', *tattvena yathā vṛttaṃ* (VI.97.2).

32. McGrath 2004. Fame is a term used in the sense of *karma ... kīrtitam* 'famed deeds' (VIII.15.1). Value is here being constituted by an act of exchange, where fame is exchanged with or earned by heroic accomplishment.

33. At the point of original inspiration, 'the *ṛṣi* saw' the poem (*dṛṣṭavān ṛṣiḥ;* I.1.47). Then later, Vyāsa, instructing Vaiśaṃpāyana, 'caused the Bhārata to be heard' (*śrāvayāmāsa bhāratam;* I.1.58).

the poetry of Vaiśaṃpāyana is recreated and rehearsed; the former sings of immediate experience, the latter recites what he has learned in the past and is able to repeat at will.

Secondly, as a subset to the voice or poetic form of Saṃjaya, the audience learns at XI.16.3 that Gāndhārī received a similar gift of divine vision from Vyāsa. One should recall that when Gāndhārī married Dhṛtarāṣṭra, the Kuru king, she bound a cloth over her eyes in order to imitate or match his blindness. She does not actually perceive anything, but sees *manasā* 'with her mind'.

In the sixteenth *adhyāya* of the Strī *parvan*, when Gāndhārī sings of her vision of the battlefield, the poet says, *dadarśa* 'she saw', followed by a depiction of the actual imagery. At line eighteen, when she commences to verbally describe this vision and is speaking to her kinsman Kṛṣṇa, she says, *paśya* 'look!' By Chapter Seventeen, this vision has collapsed—just as it does with Saṃjaya—when having suddenly noticed the body of her eldest son Duryodhana she becomes silenced by grief. Emotion terminates her peculiar visual sensibility, just as it does with Saṃjaya.[34]

Gāndhārī is then transported from the distance to be beside the corpse of her deceased son.[35] Next, the framing-poet Vaiśaṃpāyana resumes the third person *rapportage* and tells the audience, *vilalāpa* 'she cried' (XI.17.3). The audience immediately hears the substance of these cries and Gāndhārī soon reverts to the *paśya* mode of depiction, describing her perceptions and impersonating or dramatizing the voices of the various wives, sisters, and mothers on the field. She begins each subsequent exclamation with the indicative *eṣa* 'that one', as if she were pointing at the particular deceased hero whom she actually perceives.

Thus, in terms of genre and poetic vision, Gāndhārī is putting herself in the place of the royal poet Saṃjaya, and Kṛṣṇa, her interlocutor, is in the place of the old king whom Saṃjaya addresses. Both he and she receive their inspiration optically: as Saṃjaya is the poet of the battle books, so Gāndhārī is the poet who sings the central Strī *parvan*, the book of women's lamentation.[36]

In the hypothetical origins of epic song it is arguably the women who stand in the first place distributing the *kīrti*, the 'fame' that constitutes this medium: at the death of a hero it is women, who—as kin relations, mothers, wives, sisters, or daughters—sing the laments praising the deceased and extolling their deeds, beauty, and sagacity. It is these laments that later de-

34. At X.9.57. See below, Chapter Five.

35. Gāndhārī was originally at a distance from the battlefield, *dadarśa ... dūrād* 'she saw from a distance' (XI.16.4); but she is soon embracing her expired son (XI.17.3).

36. For an Indo-European view of such poetic deixis, see Jamison 1994.

velop into epic poetry.[37] Here in the Strī *parvan* there occurs such a moment, and it is notable that Gāndhārī is visually inspired despite her lack of vision, just as Saṃjaya is also visually inspired, but magically.

Continuing with the burden of this subset, the old king Dhṛtarāṣṭra is often described as *dīrghacakṣus* 'one who is far-sighted', although he is physiologically blind. His witnessing of the great battle at Kurukṣetra is by virtue of how he hears Saṃjaya sing of the events which he then pictures in his mind.

In the Poetics of Aristotle, *kátharsis* for a watching audience in the classical Athenian theatre is said to occur when the spectator imagines in his or her mind's eye events described by a messenger: these typically refer to the horrid and pitiful death of a hero or heroine.[38] It is by virtue of such *imagination*, where the audience *visualizes* what it is that they are *hearing*, that *kátharsis* actually occurs, for there is no viewing of the violence itself, onstage.

I would propose that Dhṛtarāṣṭra is in a similar position—in terms of poetic experience—as a member of an audience in fifth-century Athenian state theater: in his blindness he imagines and in fact experiences the emotions of those thoughts. What Dhṛtarāṣṭra hears—as the poet Saṃjaya describes—functions similarly: the old king *sees* by virtue of intellection, not by means of material sensory perception.

This is in fact how an audience for the battle books receives the epic as a whole, for Dhṛtarāṣṭra is the *ideal* audience insofar as he is the *first* of listeners. He is also a figure of great grief and lamentation, frequently and periodically throughout the poem mourning the destruction which occurs at Kurukṣetra and blaming himself for its calamity.

That is, Dhṛtarāṣṭra is the primary and constant voice of sorrow in the epic: in the expression of the emotion of despair, his is the dominant emotion of this refrain.[39] As the first audience to this part of the poem he supplies an index as to emotional response; this grievous and indelible sorrow of his is reiterated throughout the whole poem and is not only applied to the four central books.

According to our poetic model, Saṃjaya behaves as an *aoidós* rather than a *rhapsōidós*. He actually composes his song, rather than reciting what he had previously learned, and his speech is a metaphor of this inner vision.

37. I discussed this in McGrath 2009: Ch.V, section 5.

38. Poetics 1449b, 24–28.

39. 'Pained, having lamented greatly' (*vilapya bahu duḥkhitaḥ*), is something that one hears the poets frequently say about Dhṛtarāṣṭra (I.1.160).

Ugraśravas and Vaiśaṃpāyana function as *rhapsōidoí;* they never employ the imperative *paśya* in their declamation, for the sensibility of their performance is different. The speech of these poets links them metonymically to the words of those poets who previously uttered the song and not to events themselves. Thus the four central books of the poem and the Strī *parvan* manifest a very different poetic presence within the overall frame of the Mahābhārata, compared to the other books. This model is shaken by the fact that Saṃjaya actually comes to life as a character elsewhere in the poem when he ceases to be wholly in the situation of *sūta*.

To repeat: in terms of inspiration, the other poets sing of what they have verbally received and previously listened to during the course of earlier recitals; whereas Saṃjaya, like the sightless Demodokos in Scrolls viii–ix of Odyssey, describes the objects of an ocular field.[40] This act of representation is "captured" or framed by the song of Vaiśaṃpāyana.

This is not to say—in practice if not in inspiration, and it is important to distinguish these two activities—that in his poetic presentation but not in his dramatic or dialogic appearances, Saṃjaya does not draw upon past experience of performance; for notably, in terms of diction, he makes much greater use of formulae than the other two poets and his song is most densely composed of verbal formulae. Similes and metaphors are what come within the view of Saṃjaya's inner eye and he is constantly searching for a medium of synthesis for this vision.[41]

Both tropes concern memory for him, not only of the natural world but also of the world of poetry and myth, the rhetoric of formulae and epic procedure itself. Although, as he is describing what is *seen*, one should infer that whatever formulae he draws upon are not necessarily derived from his view but are simply fitted onto such perceptions: there is a dis-location at work. He possesses *both* a store of visual experience—metaphors and similes—as well as a bank of formulaic audial experience upon which to draw as he composes, line by line, what it is that he "sees." The trajectory of his work crosses or moves *between* the mental view and the utterance of the poem.

40. Ugraśravas speaks of this reception and its genealogy at I.1.8–9: *kathitās ... vaiśaṃpāyena* 'accounts ... by Vaiśaṃpāyana', and *kṛṣṇadvaipāyanaproktāḥ ... kathāḥ* 'epic ... proclaimed by Vyāsa'. Note that the latter is *kathāḥ*, and that the former is *kathitās*; in both instances it is Vyāsa who behaves as an *aoidós*.

41. De Jong (1985: 13) discusses the work of P. A. Grintser (1985, *The Ancient Indian Epic: Genesis and Typology*), and notes that Grintser discovered that up to seventy-seven per cent of Chapter 49 in Book Six "consists of formulas and formulaic expressions." This is not an unusual statistic for the battle books and I would propose that the figure is even higher for the actual battle scenes themselves. At VI.72 and at VII.87, the poet-editors go so far as to have Saṃjaya repeating almost a complete *adhyāya* in identical form, virtually word for word!

One assumes that Saṃjaya, as a *sūta*, had witnessed fighting before and that he had sung of this on previous occasions; for he does physically participate in the battlefield events at Kurukṣetra. As an *aoidós* he depicts what is visible to his inspiration, organizing his speech by means of repeated phraseology: a dialectic of expressions gathered and assembled from previous performances, part of his *formation* as a poet. A poet like Ugraśravas simply repeats and perhaps reformulates what it is that his hearing has received: he only remembers and is not essentially creative.

Saṃjaya renders his vision by supplying it with likeness, that is, with similes. In the central books of the epic these similes supply the bulk not only of formulaic expression but of *most* of the descriptive substance itself: much of this part of the epic is made up of embellishment which adheres and encases the bare narrative element. These depictions typically refer to arboreal imagery, to metaphorical reports of sacrificial fire, to the similitude of mountains, and to the many visual qualities of a river of death; they do not actually portray narrative moments but only *likenesses*.[42]

Thus, in terms of the poem's reference, Saṃjaya is arguably the generative *source* of formulae or repetition; that is, in an oral tradition of poetry the hypothetical proto-*aoidós* is in a prior position to the *rhapsōidós*, in terms of diachronic composition. If it had not been seen, it could not be heard.

Thirdly, we have noted how Saṃjaya and Gāndhārī—as with Vyāsa himself, the *genius* of the poem—are directly inspired poets and their song is a unique transcript representing that experience; whereas for Ugraśravas and Vaiśaṃpāyana and all subsequent epic poets, their voice only repeats a given and received script, however re-organized or reformed, of that initial poetic or mythic event.[43] The latter poets have *learned* their poetry on previous occasions, whereas Saṃjaya *proclaims* what he actually experiences, something that is accessible *only* to his mind's eye.[44]

This un-natural vision of Saṃjaya and Gāndhārī, I would submit, is akin to an "earlier" and paradigmatic formation of epic poetry, where the *sūta*—as driver of a chariot—speaks to the hero or king beside him in the vehicle

42. McGrath 2004: Ch.II, section 4 *passim*; 2009: Ch.VI, section 1 *passim*. See below, Chapter Four.

43. Experience in a subjective sense, and event in an objective sense, is here implied.

44. The argument here is slightly blurred insofar as Ugraśravas is also described as a *sūta* although he does not actually function in this role, for his poem is being sung before brahmins at a sacrifice rather than to a king; the title remains but the operation is not as it used to be. As we observed concerning the constantly changing frames of poetic utterance in Mahābhārata, this blurring of poetics is something that supplies great composite density to the nature of the poetry. I presume that this is due to the enormous range or temporal duration which was involved in the composition of the work as we have it now.

and reveals and declaims the *myth* that he either observes on the battleground itself or witnesses by virtue of divine inspiration. As we have noted, this kind of speech typically opens with the deictic imperative *paśya*, which is later reiterated for rhetorical emphasis. The *paśya* focuses or draws the intellectual eye, the mind's eye or imagination of the audience.

Saṃjaya and Dhṛtarāṣṭra, Kṛṣṇa and Arjuna, and Śalya and Karṇa are exemplars of this form of interlocutive poetry, where the addressee acts as a metonym for the outer audience.[45] The poet functions on these occasions with an accompanist: it is as if there were two figures on the stage, one of whom supplies the prompts, and then expresses a correct emotional response to the ensuing poetry.

At this point the reflections of Jean-Jacques Rousseau are pertinent to us, for he made the astute observation that poetry speaks more effectively to the eyes than to the ears: "*Ainsi l'on parle aux yeux bien mieux qu'aux oreilles.*"[46] For him, poetry *was* the original language of human beings, by which he means figurative language: "*ses premières expressions furent des tropes.*"[47] Rousseau discusses at length how this visual quality of poetry was *the* beginning of speech, "*D'abord on ne parla qu'en poésie.*"[48]

As a coda to all the above, we can thus conclude that it is Vyāsa and Saṃjaya who—in a premonetary system of exchange and economy of poetry—actually *create* value, who produce the intrinsic worth which becomes the Mahābhārata.[49] Succeeding and ensuing renditions of the epic are representations of an *exchange*, productions of something which have been *received* within that already established economy of speech and which go towards sustaining the structure and hierarchy of that system of both cultural wealth and language. In such a system values receive fungible *likeness.*

45. See below, Ch. IV, section 4 for an account of the Śalya *parvan*. Draupadī and Jayadratha could be included in this model, from III.249ff, where, although the imperative is lacking, the substance is the same. This formulation can also be observed in the Táin Bó Cúailnge, where Fer Diad says to his charioteer, "How does Cúchulainn look?" (Kinsella 1970: 179).

46. *Essai sur l'origine des langues*, Chapter I, 503.

47. Ibid., 505.

48. Ibid., 506. One should recall that Rousseau spent much of his life engaged with various aspects of musical opera. For Jean-Jacques, human beings—in the hypothetical origin of their speech—*sang*, in the sense of sonority rather than melody, in what could be termed *recitative.*

49. In a premonetary society there is no *one* sole standard or single medium of value. By "premonetary" I understand a social system where there exist no economic transactions that make use of specie. Such a system is not necessarily one that functions according to barter in a market, but one that is in accord with a system of services which are exchanged, or a system of mutual relations; there exists no market, in the modern sense of the word. See Wiser 1936; Dumont 1983. In terms of an economy of song or of poetry, there exists a system where metaphors are exchanged or transferred between voices.

We know that if there is no writing, signification in the world is very different from what occurs in a literate world and the performative takes on much greater valence; statements are neither true nor false but only effective or ineffective.[50] In a premonetary culture where it is service and not specie or *nómisma* that is exchanged, the primary signification of value of actual and fundamental worth in a community is borne by song and its corollary narrative systems and rituals.[51] This poetry supplies the ideal tokens establishing worth—a gold standard, as it were—when there exists no other primary medium of exchange nor is there any play of market.[52] Epic poetry, I would assert, both creates and sustains *kṣatriya* culture due to this activation of a system of poetically expressed and sustained social valence.

As Albert Lord has pointed out, epic functions as an integrating force for the community in which it is performed and sung; he says "we are ... struck by the conservativeness of the tradition."[53] I would propose that epic poetry supplies a culture with a common myth, a community of reference concerning value and worth, and this is the ultimate effect of Saṃjaya's vision. This conservativeness concerns the nature of verbal likeness and sustains itself by constantly drawing on this bank of repeated expressions of formulaic metaphor: a bank originally generated by an act of vision.[54]

If there exists no *matériel* as a medium of exchange in such a social setting then values must be constantly conserved and renewed, reminted as it were, upon the tongues of the poets: otherwise, being immaterial, they will cease to exist. In the model that I have just developed—drawing upon the Nagy scheme of preliterate or plural poetics—this is by virtue of repeated performance and verbal re-instatement made by a *sūta* and recycled by a subsequent order of rhapsodic poets.[55]

50. Austin 1962: 140–149.

51. To repeat: this is *not* a barter system but one where relationships of service are exchanged; there is a complementary and hierarchical arrangement at work between patrons and clients.

52. McGrath 2009, on women in epic literature and the generation and maintenance of social values.

53. Lord 1960: 133.

54. De Vries (1963: 268) expresses this nicely: " ... a distinction should be made between traditional and popular poetry. The latter always reduces the value of a song; the former derives its significance from the fact that it arises and assumes its form not at a certain moment but in a series of creative moments, and that it owes its foundation and style to the very fact of communication."

55. To be more specific, the *work* of a hero is to produce an idea, an exemplum; Karṇa, the best of the heroes, has absolutely no interest at all in acquisition of material goods and is only concerned with the production of this ideal, something which is by nature literary. His life is founded upon *ṛṇa* or indebtedness: the exchanges that he has made are absolute in his view, hence his invariable loyalty to Duryodhana. Additionally, the *work* of a brahmin is to

In this ideal template of poetry it is not just the case that a duality of alternate senses is being addressed—the visual as opposed to the audial—but that a different temporality is simultaneously being engaged. In the first instance there is a direct *enactment* occurring, with a consequent intensification of emotion; and in the second case there is a replay of that primary act which had *once happened.* To make a limited analogy, one could compare the *first night* of a theatrical or musical event to all its subsequent renditions, especially when that first occasion was long ago and presently forgotten and now only remains as implicit because of its great generativity. This chapter has ventured to reconstruct the pattern of such an implicit moment. One must also remember that—according to the poem—Vaiśaṃpāyana lived several generations *after* Kurukṣetra, which was when Saṃjaya flourished.

In preliterate and premonetary societies, as we have seen, the value system of a culture is maintained on a level of speech. The mnemonics of epic Mahābhārata as we have it now are not uniform and, I would submit, the value system created by its two differing forms of expression and emotion are various: the visual appears to be more truthful or effective than the audial, insofar as the signifier is *closer* to the signified.

Classical Indic song culture, which retrospectively projected a view of Bronze Age *kṣatriya* society, was in part sustained by these myriad reticulations of poetic performance. This process provided Mahābhārata with a force not unlike the verbal energy and tradition which went into maintaining the durability of Homeric poetry. It was the voice of the hypothetically original *aoidós* which originated and caused the dynamic value or social TRUTH for that society; and, for us today, Saṃjaya offers an excellent snapshot of such a figure at work.[56]

---

produce momentary stability in the cosmos by virtue of a perfected rite. Both dharmas, that of heroic Karṇa and that of the brahmin, are transcendental in aspiration; Vaiṣyas and Śudras produce only material objects and benefits. In the episode of the *Gītā*, Arjuna is proposing that he has received from others and does not wish to destroy those who gave; whereas Kṛṣṇa in his theophany is total and complete and abjures all exchange. These two positions represent two economic models of the cosmos as revealed by poetry. Perform as you should, Kṛṣṇa says, for there are really no exchanges; yet for Arjuna, he believes that his identity is only composed by exchange.

56. Herodotos offers a similar point of view at II.53 when he speaks of the poets Homer and Hesiod. The Indian differentiation between *śruti* and *smṛti* is similar to the distinction in poetics that I have made in this chapter but lacks the particular specificity which I have developed. *Śruti* concerns that which is sensibly received, whereas *smṛti* signifies that which is simply recalled or is memorable; the Indian tradition would not apply this distinction to Mahābhārata poetics, however.

3

Poet and Messenger

THE EPIC BEGINS WITH AN INVOCATION, which actually precedes the first *śloka* of the text itself and in this single verse the poem is referred to as *Jaya* 'victory' (I.1.0):

> nārāyaṇaṃ namaskṛtya naraṃ caiva narottamam
> devīṃ sarasvatīṃ caiva tato jayam udīrayet
>
> Having honored Nārāyaṇa and Nara, best of men, and the goddess Sarasvatī,
> Then one should glorify Victory.

This term "victory" is the presiding sign of the poem and of course, it is the one aim in life of all *kṣatriyas*. Ugraśravas then promises to sing 'the entire thought of Vyāsa' (*mataṃ kṛtsnaṃ vyāsasya*: I.1.23). This *Jaya* or poem of the Bhāratas is a metaphor of an historical event insofar as its words portray—as verbal likeness—what once occurred at a particular time and place among a specific group of people. This poem is sung *vidhivat* 'according to rule', that is, in epic fashion (I.1.9). In this chapter let us examine the connection between Saṃjaya and Jaya and see how he functions in this respect. Initially Saṃjaya fulfills the office of *dūta*, yet—as we shall see—this almost immediately evolves into the office of *sūta*, where the cosmos of Jaya is truly amplified and manifest.

Saṃjaya makes his entry into the poem at I.1.95—and at this point in the epic the voice of Saṃjaya is being sung by Ugraśravas—when his patron, the old king Dhṛtarāṣṭra, on hearing that 'the *kṣatriyas* had slain each other' (*ahan kṣatraṃ parasparam*), says to him *śṛṇu saṃjaya me* 'listen to me, Saṃjaya'. Vaiśaṃpāyana has not appeared in the poetry yet. He continues (I.1.96):

> śrutavān asi medhāvī budhimān prājñasaṃmataḥ
>
> You are learned, intelligent, wise, esteemed for judgment.

That is, he has heard a lot, he is brainy, sagacious, and intellectually respected. It is telling that Saṃjaya appears in the poem at the exact moment when the mutual destruction of the two sides of the clan is first mentioned, for this is what he *knows* about: the *bheda* or internecine annihilation of the clan at Kurukśetra. Also, he is immediately cast into a situation where the patron-poet relation is verbally established. As we have seen, no other person, except for the *ṛṣis*, the 'ancient sages', possesses the mental capacity that Saṃjaya demonstrates; he is unique in the epic, not only in his abilities but also in his experience and speech.[1]

King Dhṛtarāṣṭra is also possessed of an approximate form of divine insight: "know me as one who is *prajñācakṣuṣam,*" he says, one who has the 'eyesight of wisdom' (I.1.101).[2] Saṃjaya, in other words, is like the old king, insofar as both have access to an ability to see *into things*, a gift that in the poet's case was derived from Vyāsa. Saṃjaya's first words in the poem, spoken to his patron after Dhṛtarāṣṭra's long lament for his deceased family are *śrutavān asi vai rājño* 'you have heard about kings' (I.1.163). What has been *heard* is this knowledge gained from insight transmitted by a *sūta*, who describes in the following lines all that kings accomplish, along with their heroes.

These opening lines of Saṃjaya's on the subject of kingship establish his voice in the poem. This is the duty of *sūta* poets, to sing of kingship and heroism and to also advise and admonish their patron on the subject of his actions.[3] These particular rulers in Saṃjaya's opening song are come of good lineage, they know of divine weaponry, they are splendid like Indra, 'having conquered the earth with dharma' (*dharmeṇa pṛthivīṃ jitvā*), they sponsored sacrifices, acquired glory, then they were *kālavaṃśagatāḥ* 'gone to the lineage of death' (I.1.164–165). Saṃjaya then sings a listing of twenty-four kings along with their achievements and qualities, their *divyāni karmāṇi* 'divine deeds' (I.1.81).

Saṃjaya then establishes in this first speech his position vis-à-vis Duryodhana and brothers by making the transition (I.1.180):

> rājāno nidhanaṃ prāptās tava putrair mahottamāḥ
>
> Very great kings obtained destruction—[just as] your sons.

In these first words in the poem Saṃjaya is commenting on the end of the epic—when the sons of Dhṛtarāṣṭra are all dead—so establishing the poetic form of ring composition, which is typically how he always performs in the

1. As we noted in the previous chapter, Gāndhārī briefly approximates Saṃjaya's skills, but this is in no way her function in the overall song.

2. This is the old king's signifying epithet. It concerns not so much a sensible ability but more his penetrating intelligence; it is a complementary epithet.

3. The original model of *sūta* and king or hero is properly that of the charioteer and his patron, and ideally in a situation of battle. Kṛṣṇa and Arjuna on their chariot before the onset of fighting at Kurukṣetra exemplify this model, where the poet sings of royal and heroic duty to his patron.

battle books: those four books being *his* particular performance.[4] He calls these sons: *durātmānaḥ ... manyunā lubdhā* 'greedy, angry, wicked', saying that 'you do not deserve to grieve for them' (*na tāñ śocitum arhasi*; I.1.183).

Thus these opening fifty-seven *ślokas* of Saṃjaya fix his voice for the rest of the poem; all that occurs in this speech supplies the *type* for almost everything else that the poet speaks to his king during the epic. The poet-editors of the Mahābhārata are always precise and correct in their usage and form: this is exactly the right kind of entry into the poem for the key and central poet of the epic Jaya.

When the *rājasūya*, the 'royal inauguration sacrifice' of Yudhiṣṭhira has taken place and the Kauravas are formally received, the poet is instructed by the new king (II.32.5):

> rājñāṃ tu pratipūjārthaṃ saṃjayaṃ saṃnyayojayat
>
> He appointed Saṃjaya for the purpose of praising the kings.

This is the traditional and ancient role of royal poets, to honor their patrons with words, songs that bring value to their memorable accomplishments of rule, judgment and valor.

At the end of Book Two, when the old king realizes his error in allowing the dicing to have occurred, he is again grieving in the company of his poet. Saṃjaya's response is to predict a 'great conflict' (*mahad vairam*), and (II.72.5):

> vināśaḥ sarvalokasya sānubandho bhaviṣyati
>
> There will be a destruction of all the world along with posterity.

It is the actuality of these events that will be the work of this poet: Saṃjaya is the one who supplies the verbal description and details of this great ruin, what is in fact the substance of the four battle books, *parvans* six to nine. For the Pāṇḍavas this is the song of Jaya.

When Dhṛtarāṣṭra, in Book Three, discharges his half-brother Vidura for partiality towards the sons of Pāṇḍu, and Vidura sets off towards the forest in order to be with his nephews, it is Saṃjaya whom the old king sends as emissary to his half-brother, having regretted the dismissal of the counselor. The poet had been standing beside the old king when the latter had swooned with grief at the absence of his kin, and it was to Saṃjaya that the king spoke on returning to consciousness (III.7.2–3). The poet then performs the role of *dūta*, a personal 'messenger' or negotiator, and Vidura, advised

4. At this point in the poem Dhṛtarāṣṭra has just sung a formal and anaphoric lament bewailing all that happened in the story; this is given in a manner of prolepsis.

by this envoy who speaks in the imperative mood, immediately returns to court (III.7.15–16). Saṃjaya again performs this function of messenger with great distinction during the Udyoga *parvan*. King and poet are—during these court scenes—never far apart from each other, for Saṃjaya is part of the political coterie of Bhīṣma and Kṛpa, Droṇa, Yuyutsu and the other core Kauravas. At times he is correspondingly located when Vysāsa is suddenly present and speaking (III.30.45).

Soon Saṃjaya gives his second major speech and again it is similarly made by or through the voice of the rhapsode Vaiśaṃpāyana. At this point in the epic Saṃjaya is a mere character and *not* the primary creative figure which he becomes during the four battle books. The poet responds to the old king's desperate anxiety and reassures him of the true potential of the Pāṇḍava brothers to vindicate the insults and abjection which they have received (III.46.19–31). In a similar speech not long after this, Saṃjaya again attempts to mollify the remorse of his patron, then once more the audience hears the poet blaming Dhṛtarāṣṭra for his weakness in allowing Duryodhana to behave as he did (III.48.1):

> vyatikramo'yaṃ sumahāṅs tvayā rājann upekṣitaḥ
>
> O king, this very great violation, has been overlooked by you.

Saṃjaya constantly, throughout the course of the epic, is critical of how Dhṛtarāṣṭra allowed his son to wreck the kingdom and family: he always takes a strong moral point of view on this issue no matter how grieving the king is nor how overwhelmed the king is by the sorrowful consequences of this lapse.[5] That is, the poet is promoting himself to a higher moral ground than the king and his verbal judgment maintains this estimate of critical worth. None of the other poets in the poem assume such a strongly ethical stance. Saṃjaya assumes a moral responsibility in the terms of his discourse with the king and his patron never questions this role, always accepting the rebuke.

It is at this point in the epic that Saṃjaya speaks to the old king more in counsel than as inspired poet; the latter task occurs only during the battle books. At this moment in the narrative, as Saṃjaya informs his king as to what occurred in the forest between the newly arrived Pāṇḍavas and Kṛṣṇa—who had hurried to join his protégés—the poet says (III.48.14):

> taiś ca yat kathitaṃ tatra dṛṣṭvā pārthān parājitān
> cāreṇa viditaṃ sarvaṃ tan mayā veditaṃ ca te

5. Dhṛtarāṣṭra is typical of a *roi fainéant*; like Agamemnon he is feckless in the presence of young warriors.

Whatever was declared there by them—having observed the defeated Pārthas—
All that is known by my spy, and you are informed.

There exists no superhuman inspiration on the part of the poet at this point: what Saṃjaya knows has been derived from an informant whose knowledge is based upon what he had watched and listened to during his incognito practice. Saṃjaya relates these words of Kṛṣṇa in the first person, impersonating that voice (III.48.17ff); he then goes on to impersonate the voice of Yudhiṣṭhira, who replies to Kṛṣṇa (III.48.28ff). Next, he speaks the words of promise that the assembled heroes say to Draupadī, guaranteeing revenge; this speech is given directly but the voice is indefinite, concluding (III.48.36):

evaṃ bahuvidhā vācas tadocuḥ puruṣarṣabhāḥ

The bulls of men then spoke such various words.

In reply to this performance by Saṃjaya, Dhṛtarāṣṭra addresses the poet as *sūta* (III.48.41). This speech is Saṃjaya's first poetic presentation in which he performs the speeches of figures other than himself: it is at this stage in the narrative that he first imitates the voices of those whose words he is reporting, although his inspiration is not directly visual but still merely audial, or human; at this point he is not yet performing what has been supernaturally—and visually—inspired.[6]

During the Virāṭa *parvan* there is no mention of Saṃjaya, the poetry is solely narrated by Vaiśaṃpāyana to Janamejaya. This, some might argue, is because the Fourth Book is a *later* addition to the epic,[7] and, I would propose, becauseSaṃjaya, due to his visual inspiration, is closest to an hypothetical *earlier* telling of the poem. As we shall see, it is Saṃjaya who is potentially more proximate to Vyāsa's—unheard by the present audience—proto-performance of the Jaya than is Vaiśaṃpāyana.[8] We should recall that Saṃjaya lived several generations before Vaiśaṃpāyana flourished, and from this point of argumentation the Virāṭa *parvan* would be solely a project of the latter poet: Vyāsa has no business in this *parvan*.

The Udyoga *parvan* is where Saṃjaya comes to the fore as a character in the

6. *Sūtas* essentially praise their patrons or the kin of their patrons, and in doing so extol their heroic deeds. Yudhiṣṭhira is at one point described as 'being praised by *sūtas*' (*saṃstūyamāno sūtaiś*; VII.58.27). When, at one point, Arjuna sets off on his chariot towards the fight, it is said that: *arjunaṃ sūtā ... tuṣṭuvuḥ* '*sūtas* praised Arjuna' (VII.60.22).

7. Schlingloff 1969.

8. As we noted—or considered—in the previous chapter, Saṃjaya might really be closer to the events at Kurukṣetra than Vyāsa; in terms of the verbal logistics of the poem it is possible to argue such a point.

poem—rather than as a poet per se—for in this book he functions as a *dūta* or 'messenger', something akin to the herald of Homeric antiquity.

The Pāṇḍavas had sent their envoy, Dhaumya, the family priest, to Hāstinapura in order to negotiate with the Kauravas so that their power and authority would be re-instated, even partially.[9] This embassy had been rejected and in response, Dhṛtarāṣṭra determines to send Saṃjaya as his messenger. Saṃjaya receives a detailed briefing from the elderly king and goes to Upaplavya where the Pāṇḍavas are resident; on meeting Yudhiṣṭhira, he bows and addresses him formally and respectfully and enquires after his household, calling him by the title of Ajātaśatru (V.22.3–5).[10] Yudhiṣṭhira similarly replies in a formal manner, addressing him by his patronym, "son of Gavalgaṇi." Knowing how emotionally if not intellectually close the poet is to the old king he says (V.23.7):

> manye sākṣād draṣṭum ahaṃ narendraṃ
> dṛṣṭvaiva tvāṃ saṃjaya prītiyogāt
>
> Saṃjaya, because of dearness, I think that I see
> The king in person, having seen you!

Then Yudhiṣṭhira questions him about all the members of the Kuru household, asking about them individually by name. Saṃjaya responds with the first of three speeches (V.24.3), and assumes a moral position, and here one should recall that King Yudhiṣṭhira is the most singular moral authority—being the son of the deity Dharma himself—in the whole poem.

> yad yuṣmākaṃ vartate'sau na dharmyam
> adrugdheṣu drugdhavat tan na sadhu
>
> Since that one proceeds incorrectly towards you—
> Among the inoffensive offensively—that it not right.

He also says, informing Yudhiṣṭhira as to right and wise political procedure (V.24.9):

> śamaṃ kuryā yena śarmāpnuyus te
>
> You should make peace so that they would obtain happiness.

He instructs him not to abandon dharma, and he is speaking to the *dharmarāja*! At the outset of these heraldic exchanges, an audience

9. 'Commissioned priest' (*purohita*) is an ancient office, and is the third word of the ṚgVeda.

10. Ajātaśatru was the name of a great Buddhist king in fifth-century Māgadha. Upaplavya was the place where the Pāṇḍavas regathered after the great battle of Kurukṣetra was finished and also where they had withdrawn after their year of *ajñātavāsa* 'living incognito' prior to the battle.

immediately becomes aware of how much authority and wisdom Saṃjaya possesses and is known to possess. Vyāsa is regarded in a similar light yet Vyāsa is inhuman and possesses access to the future, knowing what is to occur in time to come. It is this comprehension of time which distinguishes the two poets yet their high moral position is similar. As Saṃjaya says (V.24.7):

> na tv eva manye puruṣasya rājann
> anāgataṃ jñayate yad bhaviṣyam
>
> O king, I do not know the future of man:
> One does not know what will be.

Vyāsa, as a *ṛṣi* and as a supernatural being—although not quite divine—is able to surpass the earthly limits of temporal constraint in his consciousness of the world and events. It is as if Saṃjaya is his mortal agent, his human substitute or poetic factotum, one who occasionally acts with superhuman ability but only in terms of poetic inspiration and not of any supra-temporal cognizance.

His message is thoroughly conciliatory and pacific and much in the manner of how the sagacious Bhīṣma or sage Vidura spoke in the court at Hāstinapura; there in not one grain of belligerence in his manner nor in his lines and his final words speak of *śānti* 'peace' (V.25.15). He says (V.27.1):

> mahāsrāvaṃ jīvitaṃ cāpy anityaṃ
>
> Life is a great river and also transitory.

Only dharma is constant in that friable and shifting world. Saṃjaya repeats this sentiment two lines later, now qualifying life as *alpakālam* or 'brief'. As the audience will hear during the four battle books, this 'brevity' is something which Saṃjaya is master of in the depictions supplied by his poetry, for the *great river*, the *mahāsrāvam*, is a crucial and central metaphor governing the poetry of those four books. Here he describes it as *nityaduḥkhaṃ calaṃ ca* 'always grievous and perishable' and also 'multiform' (*nānurūpam*; V.27.3). It is interesting that the poet views life in these terms at this point in the epic, whereas later, during the actual conflict itself, the river is a simile of death and is considered to be metaphorically running towards Yama, or Death; it is a river of blood.

In the third speech which he delivers before Yudhiṣṭhira, Saṃjaya speaks at length about aspects of dharma, cosmic LAW and propriety, whatever is both moral and ethical in the universe. He goes so far as to even say that (V.27.10):

> na karmaṇāṃ vipraṇāśo'sty amutra
>
> In the afterlife there is no destruction of action.

That is, what one accomplishes in the present world does not perish after death, the morality of all action is sustained beyond practical time. This world is the *kṣetra*, the 'field', a term that often appears throughout the course of the epic denoting the place of action or how an act is situated in time. The battle books, of course, are themselves located at Kuru*kṣetra*.

It is remarkable that the *sūta* Saṃjaya speaks at such meticulous length on the nature of dharma to one who is—as the audience well knows—the King of Dharma, the *dharmarāja* and one who is arguably modeled after the great Buddhist monarch Aśoka.[11] Of the three speeches given by the poet during his mission this third is the most strident in how it proclaims and reminds its listeners about the necessary and inviolable rightness of dharma. He says emphatically—if not pleonastically—to Yudhiṣṭhira (V.27.22):

> nādharme te dhīyate pārtha buddhir
>
> O Partha, your mind is not directed towards lawlessness!

Unfortunately the persuasiveness of Saṃjaya's poetry—these three songs of wise embassy—have no good consequence in that it is not the Pāṇḍavas but the Kauravas, Saṃjaya's own commissioners, who are in the wrong and are lacking in dharma. He qualifies *manyum* or 'anger' as *yaśomuṣam* 'destructive of glory'; yet it is the wrath of Duryodhana that is the driving fuel in the court at Hāstinapura rather than the anger of the Pāṇḍavas (V.27.23). The anger of the Pāṇḍavas is only a re-*action* to this. Saṃjaya closes forcibly with the stringent words (V.27.26):

> na ... yuddhaṃ kuruṣva
>
> Do not make war!

His last line is (V.27.27):

> mā gās tvaṃ vai devayānāt patho'dya
>
> You, do not now go from the way of the deities!

Yudhiṣṭhira replies to this last injunction of the messenger, beginning with *asaṃśayaṃ saṃjaya satyam* 'without doubt, Saṃjaya, true', ironically playing on the homophony of these three words (V.28.1). The identity is not merely audial however, for Saṃjaya, as the audience knows is—as a gifted and

11. See Fitzgerald (2004: xvi) on the relevance to the poem of the "dharma campaign" of Aśoka. To talk of the Buddhist influences on the epic is an imponderable, almost a priori way of thinking, yet it is a profoundly interesting question and similar in its hypothetical form to saying the Iliad was originally a Luwian epic: a fascinating idea but one that can only ever remain a priori in nature. The historicity of epic poetry is an engaging question, and on this see Guha 2002.

inspired poet and speaker of truth—someone who is absolutely and necessarily in his words always *doubtless.*

Kṛṣṇa now contributes a response to the Kaurava messenger, speaking at length about *kṣatriya* dharma. In the beginning of his speech, during the first three sentences he adds the word *Saṃjaya*, pointedly and cautionary, as if reminding the poet as to the gravity of the situation. He closes by prompting the poet, saying (V.29.35):

> anuktvā tvaṃ dharmam evaṃ sabhāyām
>
> You were silent in the assembly hall concerning dharma.

Thus he is observing the distinction between the messenger to the Pāṇḍavas and the poet in the Kuru court: the latter must generally restrain his personal view and yet in his role as *dūta*, Saṃjaya can speak more truly. Only in private does Saṃjaya express his real feelings and judgment to the old king Dhṛtarāṣṭra. Wily Kṛṣṇa is aware of this ambivalence which is necessarily a part of Saṃjaya's life and he reminds him of those 'not to be spoken words' (*avācyaṃ vākyam*), which were said in the *sabhā* (V.29.40). Then it was that Saṃjaya was silent, he remarks.

As he departs, Saṃjaya makes his farewell to the *naradevadeva* or 'deity among kings', the supreme sovereign, a term that Yudhiṣṭhira receives nowhere else in the epic; this is a salutation of great worth and dignity. He leaves, requesting that (V.30.2):

> saumyena māṃ paśyata cakṣuṣā nṛpāḥ
>
> Kings, regard me with a gentle eye!

Yudhiṣṭhira is utterly effusive and benignant in his compliments towards the messenger, calling him: *śuddhātmānaṃ madhyagataṃ ... āpto dūtaḥ ... supriyo ... kalyāṇavāk śīlavān dṛṣṭimān* 'pure of self, moderate, a skilled envoy, kind, compassionate in speech, masterful, knowing' (V.30.3–4). He continues: *na muhyes tvaṃ jātu* 'you are never perplexed', adding (V.30.5–6):

> marmagāṃ jātu vaktāsi rūkṣāṃ
> nopastutiṃ kaṭukāṃ nota śuktāṃ
> tvam eva naḥ priyatamo'si dūta ...
> dhanaṃjayasyātmasamaḥ sakhāsi
>
> You will never speak praise that is cruel,
> Harsh, bitter, nor sour;
> Thus you are to us the most beloved messenger ...
> You are a friend—equal to Arjuna himself!

Arjuna, or Dhanaṃjaya, to use the epithet which he receives here, also on occasion will sometimes receive another more abbreviated epithet, which is Jaya.[12]

Yudhiṣṭhira then instructs the messenger at great length how to act and what to say when he returns towards Hāstinapura, advising him how to greet and to honor individually all the members of the Kuru household, including dim-witted Duryodhana and the notable women-folk (V.30.7–47).

On his return to Hāstinapura, Saṃjaya proceeds immediately to the 'inner-quarter' of the king, the *antaḥpura*, the most private area at court where only intimates of the king are admitted, and he demands (V.32.3):

> ācakṣva māṃ dhṛtarāṣṭrāya dvāḥstha
>
> Announce me to Dhṛtarāṣṭra, doorkeeper!

Saṃjaya formally greets the old king and begins his report, first passing on the greetings and wishes of Yudhiṣṭhira; then he begins to extemporize on the human condition and human estate (V.32.12):

> sūtraprotā dārumayīva yoṣā ...
> manye paraṃ karma daivaṃ manuṣyāt
>
> Like a wooden puppet fashioned with wires ...
> I think that divine action is greater than human action.

He then says to Dhṛtarāṣṭra that 'having observed your erroneous act' (*dṛṣṭvā tava karmadoṣaṃ*) he can criticize the old king for allowing the Pāṇḍavas to be exiled to a situation whose 'future is awful' (*pāpodarkaṃ*; V.32.13). 'Understand your action, king', he adds, *karma nibodha rājan*, action that he says is *dharmārthayuktād āryavṛttād apetam* 'departed from virtue, from policy and dharma' (V.32.15). These words mark the opening of a refrain that the audience will continue to hear throughout the rest of the epic, words that are critical of the old king's manner towards his son and the negligence which he demonstrated in dealing with the truculent Duryodhana's attitude towards his cousins. He warns his patron that there is (V.32.16):

> adharmaśabdaś ca mahān pṛthivyāṃ
>
> A great sound of disorder on earth.

There are few at the court of Hāstinapura who are able to speak so unguardedly with the king; Vidura and to some extent Bhīṣma do so, yet Saṃjaya—who lacks their rank, being only a poet, an attendant rather than peer—also assumes this role of critical voice, simultaneously speaking authoritatively about what is right and valuable and what is dharmic. He is of

12. As at V.23.25. The term *dhanaṃjaya* indicates 'one [who is]winning wealth' or one possessing such a victory.

such moral stature and intimacy with the king that he is able to speak about someone—implying Duryodhana, the king's favorite—who is (V.32.17):

> hīnaprajño dauṣkuleyo nṛśaṅso
>
> Without wisdom, of a bad family, cruel.

These are not mild nor diplomatic words but words that censure in a peremptory fashion. He continues to speak at length about dharma and that which is *pāpa* or 'wrong', in the sense of being close to evil or maleficent. In fact, Saṃjaya in this speech is not actually reporting the message of Yudhiṣṭhira but talking extensively about the nature of dharma and in this he sounds very much like the wordy and prolix Vidura, the half-brother of Dhṛtarāṣṭra and senior counselor at the court who is often caught up in his own edifying yet rambling discourse.[13] Saṃjaya closes his critique with the line (V.31.27):

> sa tvā garhe bhāratānāṃ virodhād
>
> For the quarrel of the Bhāratas, I blame you!

It is 'because of your offensive action' (*tava karmāparādhāt*) that a fire burns the Kurus, he says, and 'you are not able to protect' (*na śaktas tvaṃ rakṣitum*). The primary function of a king is to protect, so at this closing moment in his speech Saṃjaya is overtly speaking in a manner that is angry and unfavorable towards his patron. In his last words he seems to recollect himself and becomes apologetic, saying that he is 'weary, agitated by the speed of the chariot' (*rathavegāvadhūtaḥ śrānto*), and is going to retire and will return on the morrow and deliver the full report. That will be in the *sabhā*, the 'assembly hall', in full plenum, where this outrage that he has dramatized in the seclusion of the *antaḥpura* will not be shown. Dhṛtarāṣṭra says nothing.

The old king summons Vidura to the inner quarter and confesses that 'Saṃjaya has censured me' (*saṃjaya ... garhayitvā ... māṃ*; V.33.7). He does not know what Saṃjaya will say in the *sabhā* and 'that burns my limbs' (*tan me dahati gātrāṇi*; V.33.10). His mind has lost its equilibrium, he says, due to these reproaches of the *sūta*, and he worries about what will be publicly spoken by the poet in the assembly hall. Dhṛtarāṣṭra begs Vidura to entertain and reassure him about dharma and *artha*, and the audience then listens to one of the counselor's tiresome and protracted discourses on the various natures of moral decorum; this occupies a long time, the period of nine *adhyāyas*. Then Sanatsujāta, a divine and unearthly figure, arrives and continues in the same dharmic vein; so distressed and insomniac is Dhṛtarāṣṭra since he was addressed by his poet.

13. I am aware that this judgment of Vidura as rambling and prolix is very much from a Western point of view.

On the next day Saṃjaya appears at the *sabhā* and for an hundred and three verses speaks in detail his message from the Pāṇḍavas, this time objectively and precisely, without judgment; this speech is a great tour de force and all the Kauravas are present. The poets lavishes great care on describing how fine and beautiful the hall is and how great and dignified and heroic are the assembled. The speech is delivered in the *triṣṭubh* metre, always a form of ceremony or gravity in the epic and a form that gives the specific verse distinction; some would argue that *triṣṭubhs* are often an older kind of poetic speech.[14] This oration of Saṃjaya is virtually an aria, such is its individual and self-contained manner and aesthetic unity; it is a quintessentially solo performance.

Saṃjaya commences his presentation—and in terms of diction, this is a highly sonorous piece—with the word *Duryodhana* 'let him listen', he says, *śṛṇotu* (V.47.2). He then announces that he will report all that Arjuna said to him, which he proceeds to do. In our present-day telling of the epic, Arjuna did not speak with Saṃjaya, only Yudhiṣṭhira and Kṛṣṇa spoke with him: so already, at the outset of this ambassadorial summary Saṃjaya is fabricating and elaborating upon the truth. It is as if Saṃjaya, for the sake of peace and order in the kingdom, is attempting to quell and subdue Duryodhana's truculence, and in taking this task upon himself—as an autonomous moral agent—is not reporting what he had heard exactly, but merely the force of those two speeches of Yudhiṣṭhira and Kṛṣṇa. He is not behaving as a good *dūta* but as a committed counselor in the court; there is no precise repetition of words as is usually the case with heralds.[15]

Saṃjaya speaks with anger in his words, language that is unlike what he heard from the Pāṇḍavas and it is as if he is trying to intimidate Duryodhana with threats of what will happen to him, both figuratively and practically (V.47.13).

> kṛṣṇavartmeva jvalitaḥ samiddho
> yathā dahet kakṣam agnir nidāghe
> evaṃ dagdhā dhārtarāṣṭrasya senāṃ
> yudhiṣṭhiraḥ krodhadīpto'nuvīkṣya

> Yudhiṣṭhira, blazing with anger, having viewed
> The army of Duryodhana will burn it thus:
> As a fire in the hot season would so burn dry wood,
> Like the black-way of fire, flames kindling.

He goes on to list the likely retribution of the other brothers, describing the

14. M. C. Smith 1992.
15. Rocher 1958.

destruction that each will render, soon closing each verse with the refrain (V.47.15):

> tadā yuddhaṃ dhārtarāṣṭro'nvatapsyat
>
> Then the son of Dhṛtarāṣṭra will repent the war.

This line—given in the *yadā-tadā* form of 'if-then'—with slight variations is repeated twenty-eight times as Saṃjaya develops the rhetorical intensity of what becomes a potent and dramatic harangue against the person of Duryodhana. He is giving his own view in thoroughly strident and vivid terms and is not reporting what the Pāṇḍavas and Kṛṣṇa said nor even interpreting what was spoken. This is a powerful and bitter monody on the prospects of war and utterly damning of Duryodhana and thus also of his father. It is one of the most emotionally charged speeches in the epic, visually depicting the destruction of the Kauravas, and all this is in the direct speech of Arjuna. For Saṃjaya is speaking in terms of "me" and "I," and imitating Arjuna, as, for instance, when he says *vidhūyamānasya ... mayā gāṇḍīvasya* 'by me—shaking the Gāṇḍīva bow' (V.47.47). He similarly speaks of "my arrows" and later of "my chariot" (V.47.51; 58), as if he is Arjuna himself and it is as if Saṃjaya is becoming intoxicated by the exuberance of his own emotions as he successfully enacts the language and experience of the hero (V.47.59):

> dhakṣyāmy agnivat kauraveyāṃs
>
> I like fire shall burn the Kauravas!

Two verses later Saṃjaya-Arjuna boasts that he is *kāla iva* 'like Death' himself. Two more verses later, Arjuna then directly reports what a Brahmin said to him: and so Samjaya, in the voice of Arjuna, imitates this further dialogue. Then this persona of Arjuna sings a praise-song for Kṛṣṇa, recounting and celebrating in epic fashion the latter's heroic deeds (V.47.64–82).

As we shall see later, during the battle books, direct speech is usually prefaced by the name of the speaker and the verb *uvāca*: 'X spoke'. Thus the song is almost a minor epic in its own right, describing—in highly detailed visual imagery—what occurs on the battlefield, and presages the kind of singing that Saṃjaya will excel at during the four battle books: what is now prospective will soon become actual and the words are similar if not identical for both situations (V.47.49).

> balāhakād uccarantīva vidyut
> sahasraghnī dviṣatāṃ saṃgameṣu
> asthicchido marmabhido vamec charāṃs
> tadā yuddhaṃ dhārtarāṣṭro'nvatapsyat

Like lightning issuing from a thunder cloud
Striking thousands of enemies in the conflicts,
He would vomit arrows, cutting bones, cutting weak-vitals:
Then the son of Dhṛtarāṣṭra will repent the war.

He even describes how Bhīṣma will be felled by Śikhaṇḍin, something that no one else in the poem anticipates at this point: either a temporal lapse on the part of the poets or an indication of the superhuman poetic skill of anticipation and insight which Saṃjaya possesses (V.47.35). Two verses later he also hints at the death of Droṇa by Dhṛṣṭadyumna.

Saṃjaya moves to closing his song—still speaking in the voice of Arjuna—with a warning, predicting how the sons of Dhṛtarāṣṭra will not survive the imminent war but are on a path towards 'great destruction' (*kṣayaṃ mahāntaṃ*; V.47.93). This is not so much a boast on the part of the hero Arjuna but more a prophecy on the part of the poet himself which he then repeats (V.47.95):

ahaṃ ca jānāmi bhaviṣyarūpaṃ
paśyāmi buddhyā svayam apramattaḥ
dṛṣṭiś ca me na vyathate purāṇī

And I know the form of the future,
Vigilant, I see with my own mind,
My ancient vision does not waver.

That is certainly true, as the audience knows, for Saṃjaya will soon—although it is not clear exactly when in the poem this occurs—acquire a divine inspiration and insight into the course and substance of the Bhārata song.[16] At this point, although still speaking in the voice of Arjuna, concerning his unique poetic abilities Saṃjaya is expressing his own words. He concludes this long poem reversing all that has gone before with the correct tone and sentiment, saying (V.47.103):

āyuṣmantaḥ kuruvaḥ santu sarve

May all the Kurus live long!

Bhīṣma immediately echoes and reinforces the warning that Saṃjaya has given which Droṇa seconds (V.48.24ff).

Dhṛtarāṣṭra then asks Saṃjaya what it was that Yudhiṣṭhira had spoken to him, which is what the messenger should have been reporting! There follows

16. This state is mentioned at VI.2.11, but it is unclear whether this gift is intrinsic to Saṃjaya or specific only for a time; for when Duryodhana perishes, the gift, as we have noted above, vanishes.

a nicely charged realistic scene when the old king requests that his envoy tell them of the names of those who are allied with the Pāṇḍavas (V.49.10):

> niḥśvasya subhṛśaṃ dīrghaṃ muhuḥ saṃcintayann iva
>
> Having sighed greatly and deeply, perplexed—as if thinking.

The poet, as if overwhelmed by the brilliant energy of his recent long performance then collapses as if he is suddenly exhausted by great effort. Or, to give another interpretation, he might simply be covering what can only be described as his duplicity in not reporting the words of Yudhiṣṭhira and for making up his own point of view. He is described, and the voice here is that of Vaiśaṃpāyana, as (V.49.11):

> ... mūrchitaḥ patito bhuvi
> vācaṃ na sṛjate kāṃcid dhīnaprajño'lpacetanaḥ
>
> Stupefied, fallen upon the earth,
> He utters no word at all, without consciousness, thoughtless.

It is strange for such an occurrence to take place; perhaps it is due to grief or to exhaustion, or perhaps the poet is merely being histrionic. Nevertheless, the moment is extremely realistic and tactfully human, supplying the narrative with a gentle pause after so much tension and poetic electricity.

He quickly recovers and addresses his patron, listing the members of the coalition who had assembled to combat the Kurus (V.49.15ff). He repeats the word *pāṇḍavā* again and again, once more supplying his diction with the force of anaphora; such a technique imbues his words with further tension and thrill as well as great rhythmic charge. Without doubt, Saṃjaya is a great performer and is not simply a messenger who relates what he has heard or been commissioned to say. He closes with the words *dharmarājo vyavasthitaḥ* 'the Dharmarāja is drawn up for battle', once again giving himself a hortatory or mantic voice (V.49.45).

The old king is distressed by what he hears and the prospect of Bhīma horrifies him especially. He voices his anxiety and despair at this and then says to his poet (V.50.59):

> kiṃ nu kāryaṃ kathaṃ kuryām kva nu gacchāmi saṃjaya
>
> Saṃjaya, what is to be done, what should I do, where am I going?

This is the great Kaurava ruler, asking his poet for direction, not only in the kingdom but also in life. Dhṛtarāṣṭra then proceeds to express his anxiety about all of the Pāṇḍavas individually and at length, addressing his words to Saṃjaya even though the situation is still in the *sabhā* and all the Kurus are assembled there. The poet is his immediate interlocutor and the old king does not address the members of his court directly but only by circumlocution. Saṃjaya replies (V.53.3):

> naiṣa kālo mahārāja tava śaśvatkṛtāgasaḥ
>
> Mahārāja, there is no time, the offence is always yours.

Saṃjaya never says such to the obdurate Duryodhana, only to his father, for with the young prince he has no relation and could be punished for speaking outrightly and critically. He is a good example of how poets became intellectually and politically involved with their patrons during this ancient period.[17]

Saṃjaya berates the old king for being such a pathetic father to his son and for behaving pitifully during the gambling scene (V.53.5):

> dyūtakāle mahārāja smayase sma kumāravat
>
> Mahārāja, in the time of gambling you smiled like a child!

This expression "like a child" he repeats five verses later, emphasizing his disdain for Dhṛtarāṣṭra. He reiterates his prophetic words (V.53.15):

> duryodhanamukhā ... kṣayaṃ yāsyanti kauravāḥ
>
> The Kauravas, led by Duryodhana, will go to destruction.

'Your son is a wicked man', he says (*pāpapuruṣaḥ tava putro*; V.53.18). Yet there is no indication that the poet is being offensive here to his ruler, and in fact this scene of almost twenty *ślokas* is a moment of emotional and personal closeness. Yet one must remember that the words are being declaimed in the *sabhā* and that all the Kuru heroes are listening to the criticism. "All your lamentation for the Pāṇḍavas," he concludes by saying, is *anīśeneva* 'as if impotent', and yet his final epithet offered to the king is *rājendra* 'Indra of kings', an ultimate ironic counterpoint (V.53.19).

Duryodhana now responds in typical bellicose and haughty fashion, praising his own companions and verbally diminishing the sons of Pāṇḍu. At the termination of his speech he turns to Saṃjaya and asks him what Yudhiṣṭhira wants and what he desires from conflict. There is not one single word given by Duryodhana that in any way indicates his anger—and as the audience well knows, wrath is the sign of Duryodhana—at the poet and all the cynical and pungent criticism that Saṃjaya has spoken: that is passed in silence. It is as if Saṃjaya possesses an inviolable status at the court and can say whatever he wishes without fear of punishment; like Bhīṣma and Vidura, even like Yudhiṣṭhira, his moral stature is highly respected and

17. Phemius in Odyssey xxii hints at such an intimacy.

authorized. Duryodhana often verbally rebuts what Bhīṣma says however—or earlier on in the poem, what Yudhiṣṭhira said—but Saṃjaya is safe from *all* retribution.

Saṃjaya reports that Yudhiṣṭhira is *atīva mudito* 'extremely happy' in his desire for war (V.55.2). This is not true at all, as the audience knows, and in fact the Pāṇḍava is extremely despondent—much to his wife's chagrin—at the prospect of conflict. Again, the poet is telling the court what he thinks they *should* hear, not what is actually correct; there is an intelligence at work here in the *dūta* and a certain moral position is being displayed. The poets or editors are giving Saṃjaya a highly nuanced and well-etched character.

Duryodhana, a creature of realpolitik, then asks him for exact quantities of force, "how many horses, how many banners" does Arjuna possess? He says rather acidly to Saṃjaya, *praśaṃsasy abhinandaṃs tān pārthān* 'you do extol those Pārthas applaudingly', for it is as if Duryodhana is beginning to lose his temper with how biased Saṃjaya is towards the enemy (V.55.6). There follow eight lovely *triṣṭubh* verses of delightful poetry where the poet describes the flags and horses of the five brothers, supplying the images with great lyrical and charming force (V.55.10):

> yathākāśe śakradhanuḥ prakāśate
> na caikavarṇaṃ na ca vidma kiṃ nu tat
> tathā dhvajo vihito bhauvanena
> bahvākāraṃ dṛśyate rūpam asya
>
> As a rainbow shines in the heaven
> Not uniform and we cannot know what that is,
> So the banner, bestowed by Bhauvana:
> [And] perceived are the many figures of its form.

It is as if Saṃjaya, warned by the irascible Duryodhana, has determined to change the tempo and tone of the meeting, and sings a delicious song about the beauty of the Pāṇḍava steeds and banners. This is a poet of great intellectual subtlety and extraordinary versatility in his skill; his range of mood and manner are constantly changing and adjusting and is always astonishing in its ways. He is an amazing performer and the poets who themselves performed the Mahābhārata must have been wonderful adepts to have enacted this character who is such a master of theatrical delicacy, moral statement, and rapidly shifting sentiment. This is all just a presage of what will be his expert performance of the battle books.

Dhṛtarāṣṭra next enquires as to who comprises the Pāṇḍava coalition and now Saṃjaya reports and at last begins to perform like an efficient *dūta*; he is precise and detailed and thoroughly cognizant of names and forces.

He also tells of the various *bhāgas*, the heroes who have been "matched" with Kuru heroes, each warrior being given a specific opponent, which provides the battle with a certain symmetrical quality. Hearing this, the old king only becomes more despondent, a mood which Duryodhana vocally disregards. Dhṛtarāṣṭra comments to his poet, who is in fact his confidant (V.56.43):

> unmatta iva me putro vilapaty eṣa saṃjaya
>
> Saṃjaya, this son of mine wails like a madman!

Saṃjaya continues with his description of the Pāṇḍavas, imitating their speech as it occurred among themselves, speaking in the voices of Dhṛṣṭadyumna and Yudhiṣṭhira in a charged and dramatic form, enacting their words of command and exhortation (V.56.47–60). In our present Poona version of the epic, the audience never hears of Dhṛṣṭadyumna speaking to Saṃjaya, and so this component of the poet's speech is also fabricated for effect. Dhṛṣṭadyumna is the hero who becomes the *senāpati* 'commander' of the Pāṇḍava forces and is thus a mighty figure.

In the following *adhyāya*, on being asked exactly what Kṛṣṇa and Arjuna said to him, Saṃjaya describes the scene. Again, he is behaving in accordance with a *dūta's* brief and his message is lucid, careful, and eloquent. He opens by describing his own modest appearance and approach (V.58.3):

> pādāṅgulīr abhiprekṣan prayato'haṃ kṛtāñjaliḥ
> śuddhāntaṃ prāviśaṃ rājann ākhyātuṃ naradevayoḥ
>
> O king, hands folded, dutiful, looking at my toes, I entered
> The most private quarters of the two divine men, in order to
> communicate.

In this rare and luxurious scene the two heroes were drunk and languid, garlanded and dressed up and indulging themselves, their feet in each other's lap. In this report, Saṃjaya performs a speech of Kṛṣṇa's, telling of how the hero-deity commissioned him to speak to the Kurus; and within that discourse is embedded an exclamation originally spoken by Draupadī (V.58.21). Next, he testifies as to what Arjuna engaged him to say.

This account is also given in direct speech, Saṃjaya dramatizing the words of Arjuna so as to give authenticity to what he had been told to repeat. Again, the audience hears the poet behaving absolutely in the style of a *dūta*, reproducing the language and re-enacting the emotion of the speaker whom he is reporting. In a sense, the function of the *dūta* is akin to the role of the epic poet, for both imitate characters verbatim and actually execute the words, reduplicating the initial setting and verbal occasion as well as its sentiment as they deliver the speech.

In all his communication to the assembled, remarkably, Saṃjaya does not relate the one material demand which Yudhiṣṭhira made, that is, the request that the Kurus give them just five villages (V.31.20):

> bhrātṝṇāṃ dehi pañcānāṃ grāmān pañca suyodhana
>
> Suyodhana, give five villages to the five brothers!

That is how Yudhiṣṭhira expressly instructs the messenger to speak to his rival, Duryodhana. This one precise and physical injunction, however, is elided by Saṃjaya, and he does not mention the five villages. It is actually Duryodhana himself when they are all in the *sabhā*, at V.54.29, who speaks of how his rival has demanded these villages.

Later, when he commissions Kṛṣṇa to be his *dūta* at Hāstinapura, Yudhiṣṭhira actually names four of these villages and tells his messenger that Duryodhana rejected the proposal (V.70.15–17).[18] Also, Yudhiṣṭhira—in conversation with Kṛṣṇa who is about to perform the task of envoy—commenting on the task of a herald, says (V.70.7):

> yathoktaṃ dūta ācaṣṭe vadhyaḥ syād anyathā bruvan
>
> A messenger speaks as he is spoken to. He is to be slain should he be saying otherwise.[19]

Thus the audience is presented with a narrative situation where Saṃjaya does not behave as he should in the role of *dūta*; he allows his personal feelings or political beliefs to influence and actually to color his *rapportage*. Then there is elision in the narrative, because the audience is seemingly unaware of how it is that Yudhiṣṭhira knows of what has been said at the court of Hāstinapura, for they have not been informed of that transaction of information. There is great subtlety or artistry at work here in terms of character and in terms of narrative, and both these dramatic aspects bring to a performance of the poem a tense charge of realism; there is nothing that is merely stylized or cliché.

So ends the episode in the *sabhā* and the old king retires in order to talk with his poet 'privately' (*rahite*; V.65.2). He asks that Saṃjaya tell him about their own Kaurava army, what is strong and weak, now placing the poet in the position of military adviser. The poet refuses to do this *rahite*, fearing the

18. Draupadī repeats this injunction at V.80.6–7.

19. The verb √*cakṣ* concerns seeing or the practice of the eyes, but in this form is indicative of speech.

displeasure of the king, and he requests the presence of the queen, Gāndhārī, and curiously, the company of Vyāsa. Magically and instantly Vyāsa appears, *matam ājñāya saṃjayasya* 'understanding the thought of Saṃjaya', for there is an unearthly union between these two figures and their mental activity is often conjoint and mutually informative (V.65.8). No one else in the poem experiences such reciprocal intellectual community with the divine sage and—I would aver—it is this conjunction which supplies the force to all of the performative aspects as well as the inspiratory techniques of Saṃjaya's poetry. Vyāsa instructs his protégé to 'say truly all' that he knows, *ācakṣva sarvaṃ ... tathyaṃ*. It is as if a Muse appeared within Iliad and spoke encouragingly to the poet, urging him to perform. Yet curiously there is no overt acknowledgment on the part of Saṃjaya recognizing the presence of his poetic mentor. Vyāsa speaks about Arjuna and Kṛṣṇa, describing the divine abilities of the latter, for Saṃjaya—true to this insight—is one of the few figures in the epic to be aware of how Kṛṣṇa is in fact a deity in human embodiment.

The succeeding *ślokas* given by Saṃjaya are in praise of Kṛṣna's cosmic deeds and are hymn-like in formulation, and it is here that the audience becomes aware of Kṛṣṇa *krīḍann iva* 'as if in play', an important concept in the theology of this deity. "Wherever Kṛṣṇa is, there is victory," says Saṃjaya, a statement that the audience now receives for the first time in the poem (V.66.9); and in the subsequent line it is Kṛṣṇa who sets in motion 'the earth, space, and heaven' (*pṛthivīṃ cāntarikṣaṃ ca divaṃ*). It is as if Saṃjaya has access to this deity's theophany, being fully aware of the divine presence that is among them on earth, a deity who has *pāṇḍavān ... saṃmohayan* 'bewildered the Pāṇḍavas' (V.66.11).

This short hymn of praise for Kṛṣṇa like many of Saṃjaya's set pieces could stand alone as an individual song in its own right. It is this deity who (V.66.12):

> kālacakraṃ jagaccakraṃ yugacakraṃ ca keśavaḥ
> ... parivartayate'niśam
>
> Keśava impels the wheel of the *yugas* and the wheel
> Of the world, the wheel of time, incessantly.

It is curious that Vyāsa had appeared in order to inspire his ritual substitute with this poem, as if the mental or poetic theophany required the *ṛṣi's* mediating presence. 'This is truth that I speak to you', says Saṃjaya to his king, *satyaṃ etad bravīmi te* (V.66.13). Dhṛtarāṣṭra replies (V.67.1):

> kathaṃ tvaṃ mādhavaṃ vettha sarvalokamaheṣvaram
> katham enam na vedāhaṃ tan mamācakṣva saṃjaya

How do you know Mādhava as great ruler of the whole world?
How do I not know him? Tell me that, Saṃjaya.

Few in the Mahābhārata are privy to this knowledge and aware of the divinity within their presence. 'My knowledge is not lacking' (*mama vidyā na hīyate*), says Saṃjaya to his patron (V.67.2). It is not only his skill in absolute enactment-in-performance that allows Saṃjaya to be the poet that he is, but also the profound and similarly absolute insight and vision which he possesses. Certainly and patently, Ugraśravas and Vaiśaṃpāyana possess such a gift insofar as they are the frame-performers of the epic; but neither of these two figures are actually characters in the poem playing various roles and they are really only—in a sense—tropes within the work. 'I do not resort to illusion' says Saṃjaya (*māyāṃ na seve*), indicating that his poetic ability and knowledge is both true and real, it is not theater (V.67.5).

This means that what happens during the singing of the epic—so the poet claims—is not artificial, and that during this ritual—and the performance of epic is certainly a rite—Saṃjaya vivifies and literally creates what he is saying: the song is a speech act.[20] All this glorification of the hero-deity, is leading, of course, not only towards the entry of Kṛṣṇa himself as *dūta* in the following *adhyāyas*—the *bhagavanyāna parvan*—but also to the great song of Kṛṣṇa that Saṃjaya is to perform in Book Six, a song—the *Gītā*—that is certainly a speech act, possessing efficacy even in the subcontinent of today—and for many people—throughout the contemporary world itself. Vyāsa himself states this sentiment, when he says to Dhṛtarāṣṭra that Saṃjaya is the messenger *yas tvāṃ śreyasi yokṣyate* 'who will conjoin you with prosperity'; this is literally what Saṃjaya is *doing* with his poetry as he speaks (V.67.11).

This encomium or song of devotion for the deity Kṛṣṇa continues for another eighteen verses, with an interjection by the old king. Typical of esoteric *bhakti* songs is a listing of names or epithets of adoration (V.68.2–14). Says Dhṛtarāṣṭra (V.69.1):

cakṣuṣmatāṃ vai spṛhayāmi saṃjaya

Saṃjaya, I envy the ones who possess vision!

After Kṛṣṇa has been to Hāstinapura on his own embassy and spoken his message and departed, Dhṛtarāṣṭra asks Saṃjaya what it was that the hero-deity said to Karṇa when they went aside on a chariot and spoke privately together. Once again it is the divine eyesight of the poet which provides him with this knowledge, a mental and visual experience which allows him to

20. Austin 1962. In a speech act *efficacy* is more the criterion at work than *truth*.

relate this important episode to the old king, for Saṃjaya was of course in no way proximate to that conversation. This is a strange scene in the poem where Kṛṣṇa is apart from everyone else and tries to lure the greatest of heroes away from the Kauravas by informing him of his true identity; that is, that Karṇa is the first-born son of Kuntī and hence in line for the throne and actually superior to Yudhiṣṭhira in the lineage. Saṃjaya was not party to this exchange and in fact the audience only listens to the event via this narration by the poet. Such is the great *psychic* and poetic inspiration of Saṃjaya, a capacity that is due to his possession of divine access to time and places that are far removed from his own personal moment. It is as if he is his own Muse, the two functions of poet and impersonal memory being condensed into his own performative action. This is the first real intimation of such powers of mental vision that the audience receives and it is this manner which substantiates the battle books.

The dialogue between Karṇa and Kṛṣṇa extends for over an hundred *ślokas* and during these lines the poet acts and dramatizes the words of both interlocutors, speaking in the first person throughout. I have examined this enigmatic and strange scene elsewhere.[21] He gives theatrical force to this production—in the voice of Karṇa—by saying that Kṛṣṇa should proceed *mantrasaṃvaraṇaṃ kurvan nityam* 'always making a concealment of their speech' (V.139.56). Such words truly empower the intimacy which Saṃjaya is projecting during his performance of the dialogue in the presence of the old king.

The verbal interaction between this hero and the hero-deity is unlike any other discussion in the epic, being uncanny and electric in its revelations of prophecy, identity, and the vast imminence of death. As I have argued elsewhere, the strangeness of this almost tragic duo perhaps comes from its being introduced at a later time, when the disposition of the poem was becoming increasingly Vaiṣṇava, although one cannot in any way prove this. It is a most haunting and eerie scene, and Saṃjaya—or the personage or voice of Saṃjaya—manages to sustain this profound incongruity, for the enactment is alarmingly absolute.

Towards the end of the Udyoga *parvan* Dhṛtarāṣṭra asks his poet once again to inform him of what is happening elsewhere and far-removed: the king wants to know what was being spoken in the two army camps, what the Kuru force and what the Pāṇḍava coalition were discussing 'entirely' (*sarvam ... anavaśeṣataḥ*; V.156.3). Again, Saṃjaya engages his clairvoyant and clairaudiant power and relates what is being uttered, declaiming the words in various kinds of first-person speech. Even in advance of his great

21. McGrath 2004: Ch. IV, section 3.

performance during the four battle books, Saṃjaya is already well practiced in not simply the poetry and dramatic enactment but in the technique of extrasensory inspiration whence his performative ability derives.

He opens the account by saying that Duryodhana spoke *upahvare* 'in a private place', once again revealing not simply the distance of the situation from where he is now but also his mental intimacy with the scene (V.157.2). He sings of these scenes with his usual adept ease and bravura in the form of many and various voices; for at this point in the narrative another messenger is being sent to negotiate between the rivals. As the pace of the Mahābhārata moves towards the Bhīṣma *parvan* and the opening of the war at Kurukṣetra, Saṃjaya's presence and verbal influence in the poem gathers force and increases. What was initially a matter of conversation and reportage now becomes more and more the nature of the epic in itself and Vaiśaṃpāyana's speech diminishes as his existence or vicinity in the poem becomes overtaken: for the great drama of the battle books is approaching.

The voices of the heroes themselves become prominent, with only an occasional first-person "moment" by Saṃjaya before he reverts to speaking theatrically once more; it is as if he is merely reminding his audience as to whom is being impersonated.

The complexity of Saṃjaya's narration is extraordinary, as he performs the conversations, descriptions, speeches—and this includes women and feminine voices—that it is as if the poet is an amazing prestidigitator, such is his great vocal and emotional range. Certainly, it is Vaiśaṃpāyana who is actually speaking, as reported by Ugraśravas, but as neither of those figures—and they are more literary components than figures—plays any role in the epic and it is as if they are mere contrivance or poetic expedience. It is noteworthy that there exists no significant metonymy in the shift that occurs between Vaiśaṃpāyana and Saṃjaya and the movement from one poet to another is accomplished without any standard cue. Perhaps this is an indication that when the epic was finally redacted and ceased to be only a preliterate text the hypothetical editors simply merged units of poetry together without any of the usual metonymies which go towards the creation of montage, or at least the illusion of montage.

Saṃjaya's final words in the Udyoga *parvan*, when Bhīṣma speaks to Karṇa are (V.194.22):

> śakyam evaṃ ca bhūyaś ca tvayā vaktuṃ yatheṣṭataḥ
>
> You can say this and more—as desired by you!

"Whatever you want to say, you can say it," in other words. This is exactly, it seems, what—not Karṇa—but Saṃjaya does.

From all the above we can observe how Saṃjaya is an active and highly characterized member of the poem's cast of narrative figures, he is a person in this process with full dramatic agency and his intimate relation with the old king and the respect given to him by the young king, Yudhiṣṭhira, reveals how central his person is in the court at Hāstinapura. Unlike, say, the Homeric poets, Saṃjaya is not merely declaiming his poetry but is a constant interlocutor with old Dhṛtarāṣṭra, as evidenced by the steady stream of vocatives which appear during his speech and the references to 'your' (*tava*) son. These small elements within the syntax of his song give the words a certain extra-viability, and make the old king a metaphor for the audience of the epic itself.

All this is utterly unlike the characterless outline that the audience has of Vaiśaṃpāyana, who really does not play any role in the poem except for the fact that he gives voice to much of the song and a certain small theatrical counterpoint in his exchanges with Janamejaya; there is no depiction of the relationship that exists between poet and king-patron. Apart from the momentary dialogue that occurs in Book One between Vyāsa and this poet-disciple, Vaiśaṃpāyana, the phrase *vaiśaṃpāyana uvaca* 'Vaiśaṃpāyana said', is the only indication that a present-day reader has about this figure, for he remains an anonymous device rather than one of the epic's active personae.

4

Battle and Grief

Central to the work of epic Mahābhārata are the four books of the Bhīṣma *parvan*, the Droṇa *parvan*, the Karṇa *parvan*, and the Śalya *parvan*: Books Six to Nine inclusive. These are the books solely performed by Saṃjaya and it seems as if there is no pause in the song, that night and day do not register with the poet and his audience of one man; although he does include in his lengthy performance mentions of day and night as experienced by the two armies. To borrow a metaphor from the natural sciences, Saṃjaya sings the element about which the rest of the poem coheres, an activity about which all worth and value for *kṣatriyas* collects. This is all that leads towards and constitutes *jaya*, or victory.

The creative effort that went towards the composition of these four narratives is massive, gigantic, and they are sung almost completely by Saṃjaya in his own voice to his apparently sole audience, Dhṛtarāṣṭra, and mostly without the introduction of the editorial headers 'so-and-so spoke', *X uvāca* or *Y uvāca*. The form is almost completely that of the poet singing the song and of his solitary audience occasionally exclaiming with grief and asking a leading question. Saṃjaya is well-equipped with martial knowledge and terminology, giving exacting details of 'tactical formations' or *vyūhas*, as well as being thoroughly knowledgeable about specific weaponry: the kind of sword and clubs and maces being used, the various types of spear or thrown missile or divine ballistic, and he is masterful in his vocabulary and precisely able to depict the innumerable categories of arrow.

These four books combine three formal elements: there are small and self-contained episodes, like the death of Abhimanyu, which are almost minor epics in themselves; there are *hymns* or set pieces as when horses are sung of and praised in their beauty and variety or the gorgeous banners are depicted; and there are the formulaic lines which although always slightly varied so that they coruscate with vivacity, essentially make up at least seventy percent of the material of these battle books. These lines are simply a patterning formation that do not possess narrative force nor supply any specific portrayal. Such formulaic iteration is what can be described as *phatic*, that is, they are spoken to convey feeling and emotion and transmit a certain stable and leveling mood, rather than conveying information as to narrative progress or episode.

If Vyāsa was the original poet of the epic, and these four books of martial struggle supply the fundamental substance of the poem, then as analysts we must consider the nature of the poetic relation between the voice of the *ṛṣi* and the voice of Saṃjaya. If the poetry of these battle books has already been sung by Vyāsa, what exactly is it then that Saṃjaya is "seeing" in his inspired fashion; what is this song of Jaya which is actually taking place? Or is it that Saṃjaya is closer to the events than Vyāsa? Due to the infolding and layering of poetic voices in the epic, there is no accurate answer to such questions; the poem is so beautifully organized that it evades precise analysis of this kind. The dramatic or rhetorical relation between Vyāsa and Saṃjaya cannot be exactly defined because the categories of speech at work are constantly changing: poet becomes actor and certain performances of the poem—mentioned in the epic—remain perpetually ungiven and exist only to be imagined.

Or, is it that—as Saṃjaya is actually in the present time of the conflagration at Kurukṣetra—he is in fact another character or one of the heroes about whom Vyāsa sings in his original song and whom the ancient *ṛṣi* is cleverly staging? Similarly, the question as to Vyāsa's place as an actual character within the narrative can be raised: who sang the voice of Vyāsa? Was it Vyāsa himself being dramatic and rhetorical or was it Saṃjaya and Vaiśaṃpāyana? The virtuosity of the epic is such that these can only remain imponderably irreducible questions; given the delicacy and subtlety of the poem, however, ancient literary criticism must surely have been cognizant of such performative *nuance* in this indissoluble quality of the epic.

Perhaps one can construe the four battle books as the essence of what was once viewed as representing an *heroic age*, a conceptual time evoked by *kṣatriyas* during their rituals; a world of the Bhārata which came to an end with secondary urbanization and with the advent of Buddhism and Jainism in the second half of the first millennium. I would submit that this *essential* time adheres about the term *Jaya*. Kurukṣetra, like the Trojan War in the eastern Mediterranean, supplied the governing signifier marking that transition from a primordial or Bronze Age world to subsequent social systems or economies. Saṃjaya can be considered as a master of truth in that he is the poetic figure or fictional device which formulates this literary and historical moment and so provides substantive form to how a new social system reviewed an idealized past. He is one who can speak of his experience and say with both precision and veracity (VI.85.13):

> tasmān me śṛṇu tattvena yathā yuddham avartata
>
> Therefore listen to me, how the battle proceeded in detail.

1. *Bhīṣma* Parvan

The first of the battle books commences as do all these four *parvans* with an exchange between King Janamejaya and his rhapsode Vaiśaṃpāyana; this frame goes all the way back to the first book, the Ādi *parvan*. The latter then sings of how the old Kuru king turns to his poet, requesting that Saṃjaya tell of what is occurring on the battlefield.[1]

Vaiśaṃpāyana opens with a vivid visual portrayal of the assembled armies and their heroes: the animals, the dust, and the individuals. He sings of how the rules of warfare are agreed upon by the two sides: *samayaṃ cakruḥ* 'they made an agreement' (VI.1.26). Then, he speaks of how Vyāsa appears and addresses Dhṛtarāṣṭra. The question is, as we observed in the above paragraph, in the hypothetical original song did Vyāsa merely present this in the first person, which then his disciple, Vaiśaṃpāyana, cast into a third-person account: for who is actually staging the voice here? The ambiguity supplies the epic with a certain indissoluble animation, imbuing the poetry with a density come of such *irrational* structure, and as such this reflects the careful mastery of those early preliterate poets. As we noted earlier, Vaiśaṃpāyana describes his wonderful *guru* and teacher as *pratyakṣadarśī ... bhūtabhavyabhaviṣyavit* 'one who has before his eyes the past, present, and the future' (VI.2.2). In his technique, Vaiśaṃpāyana is blurring his sources of inspiration, for although he certainly has no sensual access to what happened at Kurukṣetra, he dramatizes his language in order to make this seem to be true.[2] He is really only depicting what he had heard, however.

Dhṛtarāṣṭra says to Vyāsa in this opening moment of the conflict: *na rocaye jñātivadhaṃ draṣṭum* 'I do not wish to see the destruction of kin' (VI.2.7). He is, of course, congenitally blind, and he continues on to say: *yuddham ... śṛṇuyāṃ* 'I would hear the battle'. It is at this instant in the epic that the ancient *ṛṣi* grants Saṃjaya his divine ability to see: *saṃjayāya varaṃ dadau* 'he gave the benefit to Saṃjaya'.[3] What occurs within the cognition of Dhṛtarāṣṭra—he hears of the events which Saṃjaya perceives and so is able to visualize them for himself—is what happens for an audience. Vyāsa adds (VI.2.9–10):

1. This paradigm of patron and poet also occurs in the outer rim of the poem's structure, where Śaunaka, a Brahmin *kulapati* 'chief' requests that Ugraśravas sing his version of the Mahābhārata. Such an interlocutor of narratives is later referred to as an *ārambhaka* 'an initiator who helps a recital of stories to begin'. See Guha 2002: 59.

2. He lives at a remove of three human generations in time from the eighteen days of Kurukṣetra.

3. The nature of this inspiration is unclear: whether Saṃjaya is initiated by Vyāsa or whether this is an intrinsic skill which as a poet-*sūta* he possesses or has perhaps received from his father, is uncertain.

saṃgrāme na parokṣaṃ bhaviṣyati
cakṣuṣā saṃjayo rājan divyenaiṣa samanvitaḥ

In the battle nothing will be invisible
O king, this Saṃjaya is endowed with divine vision.

It is as if at this very instant Vyāsa breathes inspiration into the poet. Vaiśaṃpāyana must remember what he has previously heard and during his recital this knowledge or experience is rehearsed; but for Saṃjaya, the connection between song and experience is direct and immediate, memory has no agency in the process apart from in the usage of words, phrases, and verbal formulae themselves by which he clothes his experience (VI.2.10):

kathayiṣyati te yuddhaṃ sarvajñaś ca bhaviṣyati

He shall become all-knowing and will recount the battle to you.

The *all-knowing* concerns inspiration, and the *recounting* concerns Saṃjaya's use of poetic formulae and epithets. The former is a visual condition, the latter is aural; for Vaiśaṃpāyana both aspects of his song are audial.

Saṃjaya will not only be absolutely inspired but also, during that process he will remain invulnerable, says Vyāsa (VI.2.12).

nainaṃ śastrāṇi bhetsyanti nainaṃ bādhiṣyate śramaḥ
gāvalgaṇir ayaṃ jīvan yuddhād asmād vimokṣyate

Weapons will not cut him, fatigue will not trouble him;
Gāvalgaṇi will be delivered from this battle living.

No one else on the battlefield receives such divine protection, not even Karṇa, whom I have argued elsewhere is the best of the heroes.[4] This is of course an extremely efficacious and successful speech act on the part of Vyāsa, installing the poet—his substitute or proxy—in a unique position in the poem and causing Saṃjaya to become superhuman. In no way whatsoever does Vaiśaṃpāyana even hint at the more-than-human in his process of declamation.

Curiously and appropriately, Vyāsa reserves the *kīrti*, the 'fame' of the Kurus, for himself, for he is the one who will actually sing this epic song in its first rendition: this is how the epic phrases itself, Vyāsa is the absolute zero, the hypothetical origin of the poem, as it is stated in the Ādi *parvan*. Now he says (VI.2.13):

ahaṃ ca kīrtim eteṣāṃ kurūṇāṃ bharatarṣabha
pāṇḍavānāṃ ca sarveṣāṃ prathayiṣyāmi mā śucaḥ

4. McGrath 2004.

> O Bhārata Bull, I shall proclaim the fame of these Kurus
> And of all the Pāṇḍavas. Do not grieve!

The fame, the song, is given in order to propitiate the grief involved in the death of a hero: this is the primary exchange involved in the economy of such poetry.[5] The chariot, the *ratha* upon which Arjuna and Kṛṣṇa stand during the performance of the song of the hero-deity, the Gītā, is metaphorically the vehicle of that song, as too the Mahābhārata itself—the poem writ large—similarly stages itself, insofar as it establishes its own conditions of performance, conditions that recede towards a vanishing point of perspective or the *ur*-song of Vyāsa. It is right, therefore, that Saṃjaya, the poet of this vehicle, comes from the *varṇa* or caste of charioteers. That primary performance—in terms of the reality of the poem as we have it now—does not exist, but like the vanishing point in a perspectival system it gives form and order to all else within that system; it is the grounding zero whence all else can be *said* to derive, an assumption which facilitates the calculation, allowing it to be effective or true. Saṃjaya as *sūta* 'charioteer', drives the four great battle books.

Vyāsa concludes this brief speech with the words: *yato dharmas tato jayaḥ* 'where there is dharma there is victory'; the song of Jaya is simultaneously a song of dharma, if not *the* song of dharma. As we have earlier noted, the Mahābhārata, multiform that it is, continues to be one of the crucial charter myths of India even today and bears within its metaphors and narratives so many values for contemporary society; I would include the medium of cinema here.

The old king then requests that Saṃjaya make use of his insightful wisdom and tell of this dharma, this Jaya, for the poet is *divyabuddhipradīpena yuktas ... jñānacakṣuṣā* 'endowed with the eye of wisdom, with the lamp of divine intellect' (VI.5.8).

At the outset of the battle at Kurukṣetra Saṃjaya is said to be *samarād etya* 'having come from the conflict', and this must be the tenth day of the war; he goes to his king and says in an unusually formal manner (VI.14.3):

> saṃjayo'haṃ mahārāja namas te bharatarṣabha
> hato bhīṣmaḥ ...

> I am Saṃjaya, Mahārāja! Honor to you, Bull of the Bhāratas!
> Bhīṣma is slain ...

This formality is because the audience has heard nothing of the conflict nor of the battlefield as yet and the instant stands as the opening of what I

5. Death of hero > Grief of kin :: Patron > Epic poetry or song.

would argue is the Jaya: this is the prelude to Saṃjaya's great song. This moment marks his real purpose in the epic, not as a mere character and *dūta*, close associate and confidant of the king, but as the poet who performs the focal drama of the Mahābhārata, what is in fact the Bhārata. This is *his moment*, and the song commences not at the beginning—neither in time nor in narrative—but on the tenth day of the fighting, with the fall of the Kuru commander, Bhīṣma, when Saṃjaya actually returns from the scene of the fray. These books are also sung in the past tense, giving weight to the conceit that Saṃjaya *did* just return from the front, and it is perhaps *not* telling of what he sees but actually of what he has just seen in situ. It is a moot point because in the following three books—the *parvans* subsequent to the fall of Bhīṣma—this use of verbs in the past form continues.

He immediately sings a lament of ten *ślokas* for the fallen hero, the most ancient and senior of all the heroes in the battle and the most respected and honored of all the *kṣatriyas* at the Hāstinapura court.[6] As with all laments the deceased is praised and his deeds extolled; it is as if this small and almost prescribed or ceremonial piece encapsulates the tone of what Saṃjaya is going to perform during these eight further days of war: grief is the key. There is much repetition of the words 'slain' or 'he lies' (VI.14.13):

> sa śete niṣṭanan bhūmau vātarugṇa iva drumaḥ
>
> He lies on the earth, roaring, like a tree felled by the wind.[7]

Saṃjaya says of Bhīṣma that he is (VI.14.4):

> kakudaṃ sarvayodhānāṃ dhāma sarvadhanuṣmatām
>
> The summit of all warriors, power of all archers!

He is likened to Indra, to the Himālaya, to a lion, to the sun, he possesses "teeth of arrows, his mouth a bow, his tongue a sword," and he once fought the master-hero Rāma Jāmadagni. Then, however, the audience hears a sentiment that recurs throughout the rest of Saṃjaya's song (VI.14.13):

> tava durmantrite rājan yathā nārhaḥ sa bhārata
>
> So, O Bhārata king, he is unworthy of your ill-counsel.

These are words of disdain that the poet repeats again and again, condemning the old man's lack of mettle in restraining his uncouth and haughty son, Duryodhana, whose principal agency caused the battle; he later expresses

6. Bhīṣma is the paternal uncle of Dhṛtarāṣṭra and is of the same generation as Vyāsa.

7. The metaphor of heroes being trees—in various polysemic forms—is a trope that Saṃjaya uses frequently. After he has been felled, Bhīṣma is likened to a 'boundary-tree', a *sīmāvṛkṣka* (VI.115.9).

this rebuke in terms of 'thus your great bad-policy' (*tavaivāpanayo mahān*; VI.58.7). In fact many of these *adhyāyas* commence with such reference to the old king's folly; this is one of Saṃjaya's opening themes throughout his great declamation. Such a refrain endows Saṃjaya's song with a moral valence and force, coloring all that he says not only with regret for the weak kingship of his patron but with grief: the emotion which infuses this song which the audience now listens to during the four lengthy battle books, distinct core-epics in themselves. Frequently, Saṃjaya resumes his moral status—after pausing in the narration when the old ruler expresses anguish and remorse at what he has been hearing—to remind his patron of his own original culpability in the causes of this war and battle: *tava doṣeṇa yuddhaṃ* 'war is because of your error' (VI.73.2). Then Dhṛtarāṣṭra comments upon the seeming nature of his poet's bias for, he says to him (VI.79.2):

> na caiva māmakaṃ kaṃcid dhṛṣṭaṃ śaṃsasi saṃjaya
> nityaṃ pāṇḍusutān hṛṣṭān abhagnāṃś caiva śaṃsasi
>
> Saṃjaya, you never praise any audacity of my side,
> And you always praise the unbroken, delighted Pāṇḍava sons.

This is true, for the focus upon Duryodhana throughout this song of Saṃjaya is not symmetrical with how the poet illuminates and illustrates Yudhiṣṭhira. During the sub-*parvan* where the fight and death of Abhimanyu is portrayed, Saṃjaya certainly speaks with detectable favor about the young Pāṇḍava warrior (VII.32–51).[8] When the juvenile warrior is actually killed Saṃjaya is obviously melancholic and sings a beautiful description of the battlefield at dusk (VII.48.41–53). Much of Saṃjaya's language is in fact devoted to recording and telling of what various Pāṇḍava figures are saying, and certainly he gives equal if not more voice to that side of the warriors despite being *the* Kuru poet.

Dhṛtarāṣṭra requests, at the end of his long and grievous response to Saṃjaya's lament, that the poet tell him of the *jayam* which 'Bhīṣma is desiring' (*bhīṣmeṇa ... icchatā*; VI.15.74). At this point Saṃjaya begins his great work. This great song of Jaya formally opens with the words (VI.16.5):

> hayānāṃ ca gajānāṃ ca śūrāṇāṃ cāmitaujasām
>
> Of horses and elephants and immeasurably energetic heroes ...[9]

8. There is a strangely archaic and enigmatic statement by Saṃjaya at VII.33.4, where he speaks of Yudhiṣṭhira, Rāma Jāmadagni, and Bhīma in one breath as: *kathyante sadṛśās trayaḥ* 'renowned as The Three'. What this inscrutable statement refers to is—for us—ungiven and yet it does distinguish them uniquely and strangely.

9. This phrase depicting the three elements of battle, 'horses, elephants, and heroes',

He says that this was 'visible ... seen by me' (*pratyakṣaṃ ... mayā dṛṣṭaṃ*); then, appropriately and correctly, he honors his teacher—who is also the father of Dhṛtarāṣṭra—with a *gurustuti* 'eulogy of the mentor' (VI.16.7):

> namaskṛtvā pitus te'haṃ pārāśaryāya dhīmate
> yasya prasādād divyaṃ me prāptaṃ jñānam anuttamam
>
> I, having honored the wise son of Parāśara, your father,[10]
> Of whose benison my unsurpassed divine knowledge was acquired.

Next, Saṃjaya proceeds to commend and describe this skill which he has received from their joint ancestor (VI.16.8):[11]

> dṛṣṭiś cātīndriyā rājan dūrāc chravaṇam eva ca
> paracittasya vijñānam atītān āgatasya ca
> vyutthitotpattivijñānam ākāśe ca gatiḥ sadā
> śastrair asaṅgo yuddheṣu varadānān mahātmanaḥ
>
> O king, the supersensual sight, also hearing from afar,
> The knowledge of another's thought, the past and of the future,[12]
> A knowledge of the origin of divergent opinions, the course of destiny in the sky,
> Unhindered by weapons in battle: [this is] from the bestowal of the great-souled one.[13]

Only then does he say to the old king 'listen to me' (*śṛṇu me*), and the song takes flight with the phrase *bhāratānāṃ mahad yuddhaṃ* 'the great battle of the Bhāratas (VI.16.10). There is tremendous formality and literary etiquette or precision in all this: the honoring of the teacher, the extolling of intellectual or spiritual gifts received from him, and then the opening of the song itself. That song commences with the words of Duryodhana to his brother (VI.16.11).[14] Remarkably and fitting nicely with the production of

---

or, 'elephants, horses, and chariots', is a key phrase in the Bhārata, recurring frequently and signifying the song, like a refrain repeated during symphonic music. Horses in a Bronze Age warrior culture are important signifiers of status and valor, hence this initial word *hayānām* 'of horses' ... and heroes. Saṃjaya later sings a specialist excursus on horses at VII.22, hymning them with praise and refined description.

10. Parāśara was the father of Vyāsa and hence the grandfather of Dhṛtarāṣṭra.

11. I think of both the genetic parent and the spiritual or intellectual parent during this Bronze Age period as being considered equally ancestral; the spiritual kinship generated by the guru was viewed as equally significant and potent as any biological relation, even in terms of incest. Manu's *dharmaśāstra* specifies this at IX.235 and XI.55.

12. Or, knowledge 'of one gone to the dead.'

13. That is Vyāsa.

14. As he proceeds beneath a white umbrella into battle mounted upon a magnificent elephant he is: *saṃstūyamāno bandibir māgadhaiś ca* 'praised by martial eulogists and panegyrists',

this song, the final battle book, the Śalya *parvan*, ends with the image of a wounded and moribund Duryodhana: thus supplying these focal books with a closure defined by ring composition.

During the ensuing books Saṃjaya of course sings *all* the voices, the words of each hero are performed verbatim dramatically by the poet; his rendition of the poem is not solely a description of the combat but is a theater of one voice impersonating many figures as they speak on the battlefield.[15] Strangely, as Saṃjaya settles to the tempo of his narrative, he soon mentions that (VI.17.1):

> yathā sa bhagavān vyāsaḥ kṛṣṇadvaipāyano'bravīt
> tathaiva sahitāḥ sarve samājagmur mahīkṣitaḥ
>
> As lord Kṛṣṇadvaipāyana Vyāsa said,
> So thus all the earth-rulers came together.

This raises the question as to when Vyāsa said this, for certainly, the audience has not heard him make such a declamation. Perhaps this line is a slight ambivalence on the part of the poets, implying Vaiśaṃpāyana, who is actually speaking the voice of Saṃjaya. As we have seen above in Chapter Two, the poem states that Vaiśaṃpāyana learned his song *from* listening to Vyāsa's performance. For a small second, the Mahābhārata reveals to the audience—and in fact authenticates itself—before Saṃjaya continues in his own manner; such is the magnificently detailed artistry of the editors and poets.

The moral authority which this poet exhibits soon comes forward when he sings the Bhagavad Gītā, the Song of The Lord.[16] Insofar as he is the one to describe what Kṛṣṇa is saying and doing, Saṃjaya must necessarily therefore also witness—like Arjuna—the theophany of the hero-deity, his *paramaṃ rūpam* or 'utmost form', which commences at VI.33.9: he too must receive this epiphany. His amazingly acute vision is such that Saṃjaya even perceives the *devarṣayaḥ siddhāś ca cāraṇāś ca*, who also are present at the outset of battle, 'the divine *ṛṣis*, and the perfected ones, and the celestial singers' (VI.43.81). Often, in fact, does Saṃjaya mention these supernatural and heavenly witnesses of the conflict, at one point even describing *antarhitā*

who are kinds of military poets charged to verbally extol their princes (VI.20.7). Duryodhana is unique in this respect, no other hero at the onset of battle receives such focused performance. One wonders if such poetry was sonorous or simply rhythmic. Yudhiṣṭhira is similarly praised but it is by sacerdotal figures, priests and old *ṛṣis*, singing and proclaiming prayers and mantras (VI.22.6–7).

15. Dhṛtarāṣṭra even inquires—almost pathetically—at one point about his favorite son, asking: *kiṃ nu duryodhano'bravīt* 'What did Duryodhana say?' (VII.107.1).

16. Literally, 'that which is sung divinely'.

vāco 'concealed voices' (VII.163.36).[17] These are all aerial creatures and later, accompanied by *devas* and *gandharvas*, their speech of wonder and astonishment when Arjuna and Bhīṣma duel with each other is reported by Saṃjaya. He not only perceives these divine entities but he can also hear their voices and he says: *iti sma vācaḥ śrūyante* 'these words were heard' (VI.48.62–66). Saṃjaya even impersonates the voice of the great deity Brahma who himself sings a song of praise to the divine form of Kṛṣṇa which opens with the words (VI.61.43):[18]

> jaya viśva mahādeva jaya lokahite rata
> jaya yogīśvara vibho jaya yogaparāvara
>
> Victory to you, great absolute deity! Victory, O joy, in the good of the world!
> Victory, splendid lord of yoga! Victory to you, O universe of yoga!

This poetic and sonorous eulogy of Brahma continues for twenty-nine verses, and the word *jaya* is exclaimed thirteen times during the praising. When Bhīṣma is at last felled, the poet says that 'the earth roared' (*rarāsa pṛthivī*; VI.115.11).

At other points in the flow of language depicting the struggle, Saṃjaya often imitates the frenzied cries of the combatants, as when he introduces the brief staccatic imperatives of the warriors (VI.55.7):

> tiṣṭha sthito'smi viddhy enaṃ nirvartasva sthiro bhava
> sthito'smi praharasveti ...
>
> Stand! I am! Know him! Turn! Be firm!
> I am firm! Strike! ...[19]

Let us briefly rehearse the structural model of epic performance which has been developed above in Chapter Two. There is primarily the nameless and impersonal voice of the poet, who like the Homeric poet, sings all of the epic song; this is someone who remains perpetually unstated and undefined on the outer rim of the work, a voice without person.[20] Immediately in the first line is projected the second voice, that of the son of the *sūta*, Ugraśravas, who is singing the poem at a *sattra*, ideally a Soma ritual of great duration; that is, his audience would be composed of Brahmins and forest ascetics,

17. These become *antarhitāni bhūtāni* 'concealed beings' at VII.163.42.

18. Sullivan (1990), has shown how Vyāsa and Brahma are similar aspects of one cosmic form in the Mahābhārata.

19. 'This one is Pārtha! Where is Pārtha? That is Pārtha' (*ayaṃ pārthaḥ kutaḥ pārtha eṣa pārtha iti*; VII.64.42).

20. This is the voice—that of the hypothetical nameless poet—that is the first to proclaim the necessity of glorifying the Jaya: *jayam udīrayet* (I.1.0).

men who are unlikely to be interested in listening to a song that dramatizes *kṣatriya* dharma, particularly as manifest during lengthy battle scenes.

Next within the structural model comes Vyāsa, who is said to be the first one ever to sing the epic. On the occasion of King Janemejaya's snake sacrifice he requests that his disciple Vaiśaṃpāyana, whose name indicates that he is the progeny of 'one who protects the people', recite what he has heard Vyāsa himself previously perform.[21] It is Saṃjaya however who possesses the theatrical and poetic immediacy in the song of Jaya itself, for he is the one whose virtuoso performance and persona brings life to these nuanced voices-within-voices.

Returning to this song of Brahma given to Kṛṣṇa—actually spoken by Bhīṣma to Duryodhana, itself spoken by Saṃjaya, who is spoken by Vaiśaṃpāyana, apparently and remotely spoken by Vyāsa, whose words are spoken by Ugraśravas, and ultimately performed by the formless, inaccessible voice of an unrevealed poet or perhaps, more likely, the hand of some literate and anonymous editor—one wonders how Saṃjaya actually played or executed his task? Where in this scheme of sequencing voices was he actually to be located? Also, there is the interesting question as to what extent the poets were theatrical, enacting the various emotional states of the speakers whom they were imitating, and what—if any—musical accompaniment was present as they worked?[22] What were the visual details of epic poetry in its enactment?[23] One also wonders what orthoprax and orthodox Brahmins would have thought of a *sūta* poet imitating the supreme deity Brahma or the divine Vāsudeva? Were there liturgical boundaries concerning performance during those early ancient times?

When the Song of Kṛṣṇa is concluded and Yudhiṣṭhira, surrounded by his brothers, suddenly and inexplicably crosses the lines in order to speak with his *gurus*, Bhīṣma, Droṇa, and Kṛpa, this generates anxiety among the Kurus and the armies become silent. At this moment Saṃjaya describes not actions nor words but the actual thoughts of the Kuru men (VI.41.28):

21. Viśaṃpa, a good *kṣatriya* name.

22. The only reference to musical accompaniment with singing that I have ever noted in the poem occurs when Arjuna returns to camp after his son has been felled and the hero observes that his men: *saha vīṇā ... gītāni na gāyanti paṭhanti ca* 'do not sing nor recite songs ... with the *vīṇā*' (VII.50.11–12). Drum accompaniment is included in this picture of performance *dundubhir nighoṣaiḥ* 'with the noise of drums'.

23. In the Indic tradition there is no supporting visual evidence to demonstrate how the poets functioned, unlike in the cognate Greek tradition where geometric and red- and black-figure vase painting—as well as sculpture in stone and ceramic which date even as far back as Kykladic times—offers many instances of poetry being performed in highly presentable detail. Snodgrass (1998) has examined this aspect of the Homeric cycle.

kiṃ nu vakṣati rājāsau kiṃ bhīṣmaḥ prativakṣyati

What will that king now say? What will Bhīṣma reply?

These uneasy self-reflections continue for two *ślokas* as Yudhiṣṭhira actually enters into the body of the Kaurava army. Such astute and perceptive *inwardness* also occurs one night after the demise of Abhimanyu when the Pāṇḍava camp lies awake wondering how Arjuna can complete his promise of revenge (VII.56.9):

kathaṃ ... pratijñāṃ saphalāṃ kuryād iti te samacintayan

"How would he successfully accomplish the vow?" So they thought.

It is rare in the epic for such interiority to be depicted and revealed; in this *kṣatriya* literature internal thought or private self-reflection do not usually enter into the economy of poetry and descriptions are all objective and public, and under this rubric I would include Kṛṣṇa's theophany.[24] Fear, dismay, desire, these certainly are mentioned, but rarely are the precise words of human thought so projected by the poets. At this moment Saṃjaya says of the assembled Kuru kings and allies that, having witnessed this gesture on the part of Yudhiṣṭhira to seek pardon from his teachers before the onset of the contention, *pūjayāṃ cakrire bhṛśam* 'they greatly respected him' (VI.41.100). Again, this is Saṃjaya introspecting and telling Dhṛtarāṣṭra about how the kings were thinking: he *sees* their emotions.

He takes this ability—or this kind of rhetorical gesture—even further when he tells in Book Seven about what occurred to Arjuna *svapne* 'in a dream' during the night. He tells of Arjuna's sleeping mind perceiving how he himself and Kṛṣṇa had behaved (VII.57.2):

vāyuvegagatiḥ pārthaḥ khaṃ bheje sahakeśavaḥ

Pārtha, whose way was the speed of wind, with Keśava divided the sky.

Saṃjaya then continues to describe this nocturnal unconscious vision of the hero as he wanders in Himālaya viewing *adbhutadarśanān* 'amazing sights'; this includes meeting with Śiva and Parvatī, whose speech to the two heroes the poet sings, beginning with *svāgataṃ vāṃ* 'welcome to you', says the deity (VII.57.46). The hymn of praise that Arjuna—with Kṛṣṇa—sings in his dream is then performed by the poet. This dream extends for nearly eighty *ślokas*, unfolding into further and further visionary revelation and resulting

24. This kind of "inner" literature is arguably quite modern, beginning with characters like Hamlet and becoming very much the modal style of many twentieth-century novels. See Chapter Two above, where Saṃjaya is said to perceive: *manasā cintitam api* 'even [what is] thought by mind' (VI.2.11). In portrait painting the analogy would be when profile images become replaced in a tradition by frontal depictions, where an *interiority* can be perceived.

in a new divine weapon for the hero. Saṃjaya even tells of how, during this imaginary scene, Arjuna *manasā cintayām āsa* 'he mentally considered' (VII.57.78).

Similarly, when Yudhiṣṭhira becomes concerned about how Satyaki and Arjuna are enduring the conflict, Saṃjaya reports the thinking process of the king, his doubt, deliberation, and anxiety: *lokopakrośabhīrutvād dharmarājo mahāyaśāḥ / acintayat* 'the greatly famed Dharmarāja wondered, due to fear of censure from the world' (VII.102.8). Saṃjaya then speaks the actual words in which the king mentally addresses himself, sixteen *ślokas* of direct speech without even a framing *iti* that would delineate the internal soliloquy, such is the force of his verbal dramatization. In his thought, Yudhiṣṭhira actually imagines the words themselves with which the world would reproach him, and the intellectually agile Saṃjaya speaks these. In the following *adhyāya* the audience hears of Yudhiṣṭhira who 'having thought, mentally spoke to what was in his heart' (*hṛdgataṃ manasā prāha dhyātvā;* VII.103.32). This moment of silent verbal reflection lasts for sixteen verses.[25]

Similarly, Saṃjaya also tells of what the supernatural beings, *siddhas* and *cāraṇas*, are mentally considering: *cintayanto bhaved adya lokānāṃ svasti* 'thinking, "now may there be goodness of the worlds"' (VIII.40.115).

The versatility of this poet's performative gifts, of insight and of composition, are thus extraordinarily vast if not limitless and unbound. His consciousness, if one can think in such modern terms, is greater than any other mortal in the poem, couched as it is or embedded in the speech of Vaiśaṃpāyana. At one point of crisis the old king inquires of the poet: *kim āsīd vo manas tadā* 'what was your thought then?' and Saṃjaya describes *what* was happening in the camp, for distant events and his consciousness are co-extensive (VII.126.1). Certainly, as the audience knows and as we have observed above, the line of inspiration proceeds from Vyāsa through Vaiśaṃpāyana, but it is Saṃjaya who is the one to manifest this phenomenal presence of the epic; he is the one who is seen to *make* it real, his super-awareness is linguistically equivalent to and identical with the cosmos itself, at least for *kṣatriyas*. 'I shall speak the immeasurable hundred-thousand fights', he says to the old king: *śatasahasrāṇi ... nirmaryādaṃ prayuddhāṇi ... vakṣyāmi* (VI.44.1).[26] In the

25. The thinking of Bhīma is similarly reported at VII.107.9ff, where he is 'recalling' (*smaran*) the outrage that Draupadī once suffered. At VII.12.36ff, Duryodhana remembers what Vidura once spoke. At VII.114.63 and 67, recollection is again referred to, that of Bhīma and of Karṇa. When the three last Kaurava warriors are in hiding on the night before the Saupitaka *parvan* occurs, Saṃjaya reports what they are 'mentally reflecting' (*ity evaṃ cintayantas*; IX.29.64–66).

26. In other words, what Saṃjaya says is *Geschichte*, history, or *iti ha āsīt* 'how it was': that

subsequent *parvan* he even tells of the "spies" of Duryodhana whom he has seen, such is the acuteness of his perceiving consciousness (VII.52.1).[27]

Sometimes Saṃjaya expands and opens his voice to embrace and include others, as for instance when he says (VI.49.32):

> tatrādbhutam apaśyāma bhāradvājasya pauruṣam
>
> There we saw the wonderful manliness of Bhāradvāja.

Saṃjaya again uses this first person plural form at VII.116.6, where he tells of how "we" observed the martial dexterity of Satyaki, as if he himself was physically and personally there among the warriors on the field. Again, the audience perceives how the poet modulates his language, not simply to include others—and one wonders who made up that "we"—but simply to vary his recitative and make it more subtly vivid, bringing verve and animation to the words.[28]

2. *Droṇa* Parvan

As with each of the battle books, this *parvan* commences with a short framing exchange between Vaiśaṃpāyana and his patron Janamejaya. Saṃjaya is again said to have just returned from camp at Kurukṣetra to Hāstinapura, authenticating his especial vision with actual physical experience (VII.1.7). Old Dhṛtarāṣṭra is beset with grief that his uncle had been grievously wounded and had relinquished command. The poet tells him (VII.1.13):

> śṛṇu rājann ekamanā vacanaṃ bruvato mama
>
> Listen, king, attentively, to the words I am speaking.

The convention that a poet's song opens with a quick statement of what happens at the conclusion of his song is strangely abbreviated or compressed at

---

is the basic ground of epic reality and not the imagined or mentioned proto-song of Vyāsa, for that is merely an hypothetical potential.

27. Saṃjaya even mentions the "odor" or "perfume" that is sometimes perceived on the battlefield at auspicious moments, as when Karṇa and Arjuna duel, such is his hypersensitivity or the hypersensitivity that is portrayed (VIII.66.14). See McHugh 2008, on the use of perfumes by *kṣatriyas*, for often are heroes described as being 'with arms smeared with sandal paste' (*bāhubhiś candanādigdhaiḥ*) as they proceed to or fight in battle (IX.8.21).

28. As an aside, it is curious that at this point in the Bhīṣma *parvan* there occurs a scene where Saṃjaya describes an encounter between Bhīma and the king of the Kaliṅgas in which the former is bested and a hero call Aśoka comes to his aid. One wonders how the conjunction of these two names resonated with an ancient audience—Aśoka and Kaliṅga—and if there exists a Buddhist connection here? (VI.50.64ff). The simile engaged to decribe the Kaliṅga army assailed by Bhīma at this instant is: *kṣobhyamāṇam ... grāheṇeva mahatsaraḥ* 'like a great lake being agitated by a crocodile' (VI.50.80).

the outset of this second battle *parvan*, for in the seventh *adhyāya* Saṃjaya opens with a broad overview of Droṇa coursing gloriously into battle. 'Having seen Droṇa', he says in the first line (*droṇam ... dṛṣṭvā*), which is the usual form, but by line twenty-nine he is saying *droṇo gataḥ svargam* 'Droṇa has gone to heaven', meaning that he is dead. Saṃjaya has just compressed what will become one hundred and seventy-three *adhyāyas* into these few *ślokas*. As usual, once the eponymous hero is dead, the poet, on being asked by his grieving interlocutor what happened, then enters or opens the narrative proper. This is the poetic technique: so-and-so is no more, which elicits despair on the part of an audience, and thence the rest of the narration becomes a retrojection depicting 'how' (*katham*) this heroic demise occurred. It is as if the narrative, by convention, must loop backwards at certain defining points where a new stage is embarked upon, and only then might it proceed as before in linear time; this is an efficient way to impart ring composition to the work.[29]

Overwhelmed by despondency and gloom, the old king actually loses consciousness and faints upon the ground. Notably, it is the Bhārata women—who are said to be present—who restore him, implying that these silent women must have been present during the performance of Saṃjaya's song of Bhīṣma (VII.9.3ff). Alert once more, Dhṛtarāṣṭra again requests that the poet tell of how Droṇa perished; in doing this he praises the hero at great length himself, singing his own litany of admiration for Droṇa and an heroic depiction of his assailants which extends for more than an hundred *ślokas*, most of which are interrogative towards the poet. Then Saṃjaya says: *pāṇḍavās tu jayaṃ labdhvā* 'the Pāṇḍavas, having seized victory', and so he begins to sing the Droṇa song, the word *jaya* having, as we observed earlier, acted as the trigger for the onset of this song. He makes the uncommon claim: *te varṇayiṣyāmi sarvaṃ pratyakṣadarśivān* 'I, who have seen what is visible to the soul, shall paint all for you' (VII.11.1).[30]

As Saṃjaya depicts the long battles and duels of this *parvan*, at one moment when Arjuna is raging about the field the poet says: *nāpaśyāma ... sainyaṃ tamasāvṛtam* 'we did not see the army covered in darkness', and he says (VII.29.31):

> gāṇḍīvasya ca nirghoṣo śruto dakṣiṇato mayā
>
> The noise of the Gāṇḍīva-bow was heard by me from the south.

29. The sub-*parvan* describing the death of Abhimanyu also begins in this reverse-circular fashion, with the poet stating that Arjuna's son had been killed at VII.32.20, followed by the expression of the old king's sorrow and then his plea to hear *how* this occurred. Ring composition is definitely the mode of this epic's core scenes.

30. The verb √*varṇ* means to dye or to paint, to depict.

Two lines later, in all this shroud of darkness and dust generated by combat, Saṃjaya adds that: *droṇam anvagām* 'I followed Droṇa'.

Whether this would indicate his material presence on the field or whether this is a rhetorical and theatrical gesture, imparting a savor of reality for the audience, cannot be determined. It is typical of the subtlety of Saṃjaya, however, that he plays with sensual perception and presence in this manner: the style of slight statements charges the poetry with vitality, for Saṃjaya's own body is thus more closely engaged in the drama, he is not merely a super-camera with telescopic lenses recording what occurs within his magical sight.

He speaks in a similar *instantaneous* fashion immediately after the slaying of Abhimanyu when he says: *niveśāyābhyupāyāma sāyāhne* 'we returned to camp in the evening', supplying the words with a supplement that gives further sense of the genuine and a dimension of what is nowadays called *real time*: his super-vision allows him to actually be materially present at certain scenes (VII.48.39). Saṃjaya speaks about 'we' (*vayam*) as they return exhausted to camp, being observed by the enemy, and it is as if he is so caught up by his vision that he participates in the field himself. Such a moment of empathy—if not actuality—he repeats later when he says that: *vayaṃ droṇaṃ puraskṛtya* 'we, having put Droṇa to the fore' (VII.70.6). This ambiguity of presence by the narrator only serves to invigorate the movement of his song and its veracity is insignificant. So personally involved he is soon saying (VII.70.41):

> svakenāham anīkena saṃnaddhakavacāvṛtaḥ
> catuḥśatair maheṣvāsaiś cekitānam avārayam
>
> I, covered with an armed cuirass, with my own army,
> Restrained Cekitāna with four hundred great archers.

This fusion which occurs between Saṃjaya's song and his own presence *within* the battle scenes again resurfaces at a later point, when the poet remarks to the old king, in answer to a question (VII.157.19):

> duryodhanasya śakuner mama duḥśānasya ca
> rātrau rātrau bhavaty eṣā nityam eva samarthanā
>
> Night after night this is always our concern,
> Of Duśāsana, of myself, of Śakuni, and of Duryodhana ...

Saṃjaya is indicating his own personal presence within the song itself, a presence that is unseen upon the surface of the song, and his use of the present tense in this statement gives the claim force. It is a sign of the fine subtlety and artistry of these poet-editors who are constantly playing with such delicate nuance in the diction of the epic and hence supplying it with a tremendous *reality*.

In the voice of Arjuna, Saṃjaya sings in full mourning pathos a father's lament for a son, a song that is formally akin to the laments which are sung during the Strī *parvan* (VII.50.23ff). Saṃjaya then sings another lament for Abhimanyu five *adhyāyas* later, this time in the person of his young and desperate mother, Subhadrā (VII.55.2ff). The words of the poet during these moments of blind anguish and tears—Subhadrā is singing this in the presence of her brother, Kṛṣṇa—must have been intensely moving for an audience. One wonders as to the conventional physical gestures which might have accompanied these signs of grief which are like operatic arias in their pitiful tendentiousness: how would Saṃjaya have performed this feminine and sorrowing person? The moment is unique in the battle books, where the feminine voice and image are almost completely—except for a couple of minor similes—excluded.

I am reminded of something that Gregory Nagy once said when discussing the theatrical and expressive ability that these ancient poets possessed as they ran through—during their performances—the gamut of human emotion: "You don't have to have the blues to sing the blues," he commented.[31] Grief and the expression of grief are perhaps the most intrinsic emotions that epic makes manifest and for poets to perform such states—in this case the great Arjuna, overwhelmed by sudden profound and inalienable despair—required extraordinary artistic gifts. This is not the kind of verse that editors can tamper with or change, and it is the kind of poetry that only comes truly alive during performance.[32]

It is remarkable that when Dhṛtarāṣṭra first begins to sense that there is a crisis in the camp he describes to Saṃjaya the *absence* of sounds, the lack of singing and playing of musical instruments and the silence of human voices in dispute; he depicts the individual tents of his kinfolk, and queries their quietness. Nothing visual is given for he is, of course, blind (VII.61). One line of his speech reminds me of the victory odes of Pindar, sung to celebrate the return of an heroic athlete from the games (VII.61.7):

> stuvatāṃ nādya śrūyante putrāṇāṃ śibire mama
> sūtamāgadhasaṃghānāṃ nartakānaṃ ca sarvaśah
>
> Now the praising of my sons is not heard in the camp,
> Of dancers, of eulogists and poets, anywhere.[33]

31. Nagy 2004b.

32. Grief is of course the natural obverse to love. In the epic the emotion of love is scarcely addressed other than in this obverse form: there exists this constant ellipsis.

33. The *sūta* is a personal poet and also one to accompany a hero on his chariot in battle;

It is rare in the epic for the pleasures of heroes to be described, and in this *adhyāya*—in their absence—the delights of camp life are hinted at by the old king, who is worried because he can no longer hear those sounds. One wonders if this is a slip or nod on the part of the poets, for it always seemed that Dhṛtarāṣṭra and Saṃjaya were physically far removed from the scene of Kurukṣetra and it was only the poet's super-sensibility that allowed him to perceive the action. The reference to *saṃgha* 'group' is perhaps an indication of chorus, who might be accompanying the *nartakās*, the 'dancers'.

As the great and vindictive pursuit begins where Arjuna finally catches up with Jayadratha, the hero who orchestrated the death of Abhimanyu, Saṃjaya opens this *adhyāya* with more than his usual injunction to the old king, as if enjoining his audience with the importance and wonder of this duel. He says: *śṛṇu kīrtayato mama ... yuddham*, 'listen to my making famous the fight' (VII.71.1). The word *kīrti* 'fame' is a term that encapsulates the oral tradition of epic poetry: this is something that heroes receive for valor if not death in battle and such a form of praise commemorating this fame is intrinsic to the nature and composition of epic song.[34] It is rare for Saṃjaya to accent his production with such a statement—that he will now *make famous* this especial duel—bringing a particular surcharge to his words.[35] If one were to actually define epic poetry and production the word *kīrtayati* 'he makes fame' would succinctly capture this verbal and literary activity. This is essentially what happens in or *with* the battle books, and is what the poet Saṃjaya is *doing*.

When the pursuit of Jayadratha approaches terminus there occurs a hiatus in the progress of the narrative, for the old king asks his poet to 'make visible the standards for me' (*dhvajān ... tān mamācakśva*). A complete *adhyāya* is then devoted to Saṃjaya's visualizing the banners for his patron; he commences (VII.80.2):

> rūpato varṇataś caiva nāmataś ca nibodha me
>
> Learn from me the names, colors, and forms ...

---

māgadha is usually translated by the word 'eulogist', a personal praise poet or one who sings hymns and encomia for elite individuals; there also exists the *bandin*, a more 'martial poet', one who sings as he accompanies a fighting force into battle, something like a Greek *paián* perhaps? Pindar's victory odes were songs that were performed by a choral group celebrating the *nostos*, the 'return' of a successful athlete from the games. Athletics in Hellenic society recapitulated the ordeals and trials of heroes in battle and took their hypothetical origin from the funeral games. See Nagy 1990; Kurke 1991. 'Musical instruments' (*vāditras*) are also mentioned at VII.60.20; at IX.7.4 these instruments are *bodhanārthaṃ hi yodhānāṃ* 'for the purpose of arousing the warriors'.

34. McGrath 2004: Chapter 2.

35. As the soundtrack in contemporary cinema can surcharge or emphasize the especial drama of a scene with a particular kind of musical accompaniment or change in musical tempo.

'Then those flags were seen dancing, stirred by the air' (*patākāś ca tatas tās tu śvasanena samīritāḥ nṛtyamānā vyadṛśyanta*; VII.80.6). In a song of ekphrasis he lists ten individual insignias flown by the heroes, each one being a visible image. That of Jayadratha is unusual for it depicts a divine figure: one thinks of visual representation in general, and not just of divinities in particular, as historically only beginning at the time of the Aśokan capitals. It is (VII.80.19):

> sā sītā bhrājate tasya ratham āsthāya māriṣa
> sarvabījavirūḍheva yathā sītā śriyā vṛtā
>
> Sītā sparkled, mounted on her chariot, sir,
> The thriver of all seed: so Sītā, prosperously enveloped.[36]

Atop this particular banner, *dvajāgre* a 'silvery boar', *varāhaḥ ... rājato* was shining, 'embellished with a network of gold' (*hemajālapariṣkṛtaḥ*).[37] Curiously, Saṃjaya portrays the standards of nine Kuru leaders and that of Arjuna but he omits all mention of Duryodhana's emblem, although the son of Dhṛtarāṣṭra is at the head of his force. This hymn to the *dvajas* stands apart from the ongoing progress of the narrative; it is like the hymn to the horses at VII.22, functioning as a lovely interlude in the battle, when Saṃjaya makes visible a specific detail or summary of detail of the overall scene.[38] It is a sudden, virtuoso, and extended view of that which is beautiful rather than gory and brutal.[39]

Now occurs something in the verses of this *parvan* that seriously broaches the rigor of my argument concerning the distinction between the poetics of Saṃjaya and Vaiśaṃpāyana. As it only happens once—to my knowledge—the argument remains standing but with this sole exception. In *adhyāya* 89, which is spoken by Dhṛtarāṣṭra, there is a reduplication of not simply phrases or formulae but of a complete series of *ślokas* which have been spoken before by the old king in the Bhīṣma *parvan* 72. There is even the image, identical in both speeches, of the ocean to which the river of death or battle runs (VII.89.11):

36. "Personified, and apparently once worshipped as a kind of goddess resembling Pomona; in RV IV.57.6, Sītā is invoked as presiding over agriculture or the fruits of the earth"; Monier Williams.

37. In the West, the boar was often associated with Demeter, also a cereal divinity.

38. In the sense made by the word *bilden* 'giving shape'.

39. The long and exquisitely poetic portrayal of horses is to be found at VII.22.2–63. The steeds of Nakula are said to be *darśanīyās tu kāmbojāḥ śukapatraparicchadāḥ* 'of the Kamboja breed, lovely, decked with feathers of parrot' (22.3). Horses are portrayed as 'bearing necklaces of gold' (*rukmamālādharāḥ*; 22.31); or being 'the color of a red moon' (*śaśalohitavarṇās*; 22.43); or 'colored as blue lotos' (*nīlotpalasavarṇās*; 22.51). This lovely song extolling the details of equine beauty is a distinct work of poetry in itself and sounds as if it was once a separate piece of verse.

mahodadhim ivāpūrṇam āpagābhiḥ samantataḥ
apakṣaiḥ pakṣisaṃkāśai rathair aśvaiś ca saṃvṛtam

Like a great sea full with rivers on all sides,
Provided with horses and chariots, wingless yet as if winged.[40]

What is occurring in the usage of this passage? Dhṛtarāṣṭra tells of what he is seeing, and of course, he is blind. He describes the *vyūha*, the 'tactical array' and how it appears visually; then follows this simile, how the force is *like* an ocean and his images are immediately perceptible. Something is wrong, for he can see nothing, even though he does say *na paśyāmi* 'I do not see', referring to his anticipation for his troop's survival in defeat (VII.89.16).[41] It is as if the poets or editors have nodded and given him a speech of Saṃjaya's and it is anomalous that the similar and in part identical speech occurs in a previous chapter, also in the voice of Dhṛtarāṣṭra. If there is no error and the words ring true, being spoken by Vaiśaṃpāyana, then my argument concerning the distinction of *aoidós* and *rhapsōidós* collapses, at least in this sole instance, insofar as the distinction between the voices and speech of Saṃjaya and Vaiśaṃpāyana are conflated. I think that the problem is editorial though, and not poetic, and so the argument holds.

This speech proceeds and becomes somewhat similar to a speech delivered by the old king to his poet in the Ādi *parvan*, right at the beginning of the epic.[42] There the reiterated words *yadāśrauṣam* 'when I heard' receive the repeated correlative *tadā nāśaṃse vijayāya* 'then I did not hope for victory' (I.1.102ff). In this present speech to his poet, Dhṛtarāṣṭra begins a clause: *dṛṣṭvā* 'having seen' and then having depicted an object, the correlative is *manye śocanti putrakāḥ* 'I think my sons grieve' (VII.89.30ff). This paradigm of diction is repeated eight times.

Something about this speech, or both sections of the speech, is slightly awry and does not accord with the usual or common organization of enunciation that occurs between these two figures, king and poet. It would appear that the attention of the editor-poets has slipped in temperament here. The manner of the narrative, however, soon reverts to its usual form with the poet imitating the words and cries of heroes on the field as they struggle, and Saṃjaya is again saying 'I have seen a marvel there' (*tatrādbhutaṃ ... dṛṣṭavān asmi*; VII.98.29).

Once Bhīṣma has fallen and then the heroes Jayadratha and Bhūriśravas have been decapitated, a despondency begins to settle on the Kaurava

40. In the Bhīṣma *parvan* this exact extended simile begins at 72.14.

41. He repeatedly uses the words *paśyāmi* or *pratipaśyāmi* at the beginning of VII.115, with this sense of anticipation rather than of perception.

42. Let us recall that Vaiśaṃpāyana has not entered the epic at this point.

leaders. There ensues a *rātriyuddha* 'a battle at night', during which Saṃjaya continues to portray events with his usual minute detail even though all is thoroughly dark, such are his powers of viewing. Dhṛtarāṣṭra inquires not "what did you see" nor "what happened," but: *kā vo'bhūd vai matis tadā* 'what was your thought then?' (VII.130.1). It is within his mind that all this conflict occurs and these unilluminated night scenes are particularly ghastly, being *timiraghanair ivāvṛtaṃ* 'enveloped with dense darkness' (VII.130.40). Saṃjaya perceives all, even though (VII.147.20):

> tamasā saṃvṛte loke na prājñāyata kiṃcana
>
> When the world was enveloped with darkness nothing could be discerned.

This inspissate murkiness re-occurs later towards the end of the night as the sun is arising through dust, for then (VII.161.17):

> naiva te na vayaṃ rājan prajñāsiṣma parasparam
>
> O king, neither they nor we distinguished each other.

All the combatants become *muḍham ... andham* 'stupefied, blind', yet nevertheless, Saṃjaya's acute magical perception continues to function. It is noteworthy that the first person plural used in this line implies that he himself was present within that mineral haziness of dawn; Saṃjaya does not usually employ that form of person simply to signify the Kauravas.[43]

More than this, the poet's super-sensibility perceives the sound of (VII.147.35):

> aśrūyanta hi nāmāni śrāvyamāṇāni pārthivaiḥ
> praharadbhir mahārāja svayaṃvara ivāhave
>
> Mahārāja, names being announced by the champion
> Princes, were heard in battle, as in a bride-choice.

Similarly, just after a long duel in this *parvan* has concluded, a long nighttime scene which Saṃjaya has visually portrayed during the course of two *adhyāyas*, the poet then comments on the audible aspects of the moment (VII.153.34):

> tato bherīsahasrāṇi śaṅkhānām ayutāni ca
> avādayan pāṇdaveyās tasmin rakṣasi pātite
>
> Then thousands of drums and myriads of conches
> The Pāṇdavas sounded, when that *rakṣasa* was felled.

43. When the decapitated Droṇa's spirit ascends into the sky like a meteor, Saṃjaya uses this unusual first person plural form again: *apaśyāma* 'we saw' (VII.165.57).

Audial perception is the "marked" ability and the visual skill of the poet is the unmarked sensation: for Vyāsa gave him this superhuman capacity only in the visible field, so the poem claims; but this in fact includes sounds as well as sights.

Soon the ancient *ṛṣi* re-emerges to console and to encourage the waning spirit of Yudhiṣṭhira, who is filled with despond at the death of his young nephew. Suddenly, without any prior indication, Vyāsa is within the narrative and speaking, and Saṃjaya continues with his song merely with the words: *abhigamyābravīt vyāso* 'Vyāsa having approached said' (VII.158.53). Now, it is Saṃjaya who reports what Vyāsa, the *ur*-poet, said! Such is the great involution of poetics that the literal structure of the poem becomes thoroughly—due to this irrationality—elusive, or, cleverly made to be fully unrevealing of its internal self.

Vyāsa speaks to Yudhiṣṭhira and deflects the Pāṇḍava king's present course of action: Yudhiṣṭhira ceases to pursue Karṇa, and it is Vyāsa who has caused this. The poet then gives in direct speech those words of his mentor and inspirer, mantic words in which the old sage prophesies to the Dharmarāja that victory will be his in five days.[44] Saṃjaya is thus simultaneously prophesying to Dhṛtarāṣṭra that the Kauravas will be defeated within five days. It is as if the dimensions of the epic suddenly take on dual form, or as if the vanishing point of the narrative's perspective shifts from one situation to another: this is what Vyāsa accomplishes in the poem, for his intrusive and simultaneously creative figure causes various narratives to fuse into each other and simultaneously combine as the battle progresses. With the words: *yato dharmas tato jayaḥ* 'where dharma exists there is *Jaya*', *vyāsas tatraivāntaradhīyata* 'Vyāsa there vanished' (VII.158.62).[45] The *ṛṣi* becomes invisible, submerged within the narrative once again; for like Saṃjaya, he is both composer and actor, performer and performed. The only difference between these two figures is that Vyāsa is genetically connected with the two rival sides of the clan, being the biological grandfather of both Yudhiṣṭhira and Duryodhana.[46] Vyāsa's affiliation is lineal whereas Saṃjaya's is loyal.

Just as the *ṛṣi* Vyāsa appeared out of the air, so too, as Droṇa is about to succumb and perish, many other great Vedic *ṛṣis* suddenly materialize:

44. I assume that here Saṃjaya is describing an event in which Vyāsa appears on the battlefield. Logically, in terms of poetics, this presents a problem for the scheme that we have proposed, where Vyāsa is the *ur*-speaker of the epic; it does make for a more seamless poem however.

45. To repeat, Saṃjaya's words are the medium or the record of this dharma: that is *the epic of Jaya*.

46. Bhīṣma is always referred to as a paternal 'grandfather' (*pitāmaha*) even though he is in fact a great-uncle.

Viśvāmitra, Jamadagni, Bharadvāja, Gautama, Vasiṣṭha, Kaśyapa, Atri, are all there and observed by Saṃjaya (VII.164.87). They warn Droṇa of his imminent demise, and Saṃjaya—given his supersensible perception—of course gives voice to their speech, imitating the *quasi*-divinities.

At the conclusion of the Droṇa *parvan* Vyāsa materializes once more, this time in order to speak with the son of Droṇa. During these words, Vyāsa reports what blue-throated Śiva, as Śaṃkara, himself once said. Both speeches—that of the *ṛṣi* and of the deity—are given by Saṃjaya, a tour de force which brings majestic closure to this terrific book, perhaps the most violent and complex of all the battle books. Vyāsa sings a long hymn in praise of Rudra and his ontogeny, then: *jagāma ... yathāgatam* 'he departed as he arrived'.[47] Saṃjaya employs his mentor and *guru* to supply closure to these five days of savage and awful conflict in this resounding poetic flourish of conclusion.[48] From this point onwards the battle becomes less magnificent and more human, without the two great warrior-heroes, Bhīṣma and Droṇa, to direct events.

3. *Karṇa* Parvan

As with the two previous battle books there is no hiatus in the poetry between Books Seven and Eight; there is mention of the armies and warriors occasionally sleeping or taking rest, but there is no indication of such respite in the long conversation between Dhṛtarāṣṭra and Saṃjaya. Many tens of hours have gone into the performance so far yet there is no hint as to duration or lapse apart from the *adhyāyas*, and one wonders how in fact the poetry was organized as a performance in terms of time. In temple recitals of the Mahābhārata that I have witnessed in western India today, it is the arrival of late evening that leads to the close of a particular *adhyāya*, bringing with it a terminus to the day's singing.

As usual with the opening of a battle book, Vaiśaṃpāyana speaks to his patron, Janamejaya, and introduces Saṃjaya and the old king, once more establishing the situation between these two interlocutors. As we have previously observed this manner of a king asking a question of his poet who then proceeds to perform is very much the general and overall form of the epic and nature of its founding rhetoric. Also, the opening manner is always

47. This hymn stands apart from the rest of the *parvan* as if it had been added at a later date in the history of the poem; it was not unusual for such additions to be placed at the *end* of a section. However, S. K. De in his Appendix to the second volume of the Poona CE Droṇa *Parvan* (1958: 1158), notes that contrary to such views—by scholars like Hopkins—this hymn is present in *both* the Northern and Southern Recensions, indicating an early provenance.

48. The spectacular deaths of Abhimanyu, Jayadratha, Ghaṭotkaca, and Droṇa himself, distinguish this *parvan*.

the same: the poet pronounces the hero fallen and the king inquires as to 'how' (*katham*) this occurred.

Vaiśaṃpāyana then says that when Karṇa was killed, Saṃjaya returned from the combat towards the palace at Hāstinapura: *niśi ... dīno yayau nāgapuram aśvair vātasamair jave* 'downcast, he went in the night towards Hāstinapura with horses like the wind in velocity' (VIII.1.25). Implicit in this statement is that Saṃjaya was present on the battlefield at Kurukṣetra and was *not* simply viewing the fray from a distance employing his divine vision; thus the poet-editors again blur his situation of telepathy and physical presence. Vaiśaṃpāyana begins by saying that the poet greets the old king in a manner that the audience has previously heard at the outset of the first battle book: *saṃjayo'haṃ* 'I am Saṃjaya' (VIII.1.29). Then the dialogue between the two commences. After being critical—as usual—of the king's policy which had led to and caused all this great internecine carnage, he says (VIII.2.9):

> jayo vāpi vadho vāpi yudhyamānasya saṃyuge / bhavet ...
>
> Of one fighting in battle there would be either victory or annihilation.

Annihilation is death as we have seen or heard, and victory is its correlative; they are simultaneously activated in the song itself via the poetry of Saṃjaya, hence the early title of the epic as Jaya; for these two events, death and the song, are merely obverse and reverse of one occurrence.

Saṃjaya now says to Dhṛtarāṣṭra, but as if he is standing beside Duryodhana on a chariot—where a *sūta* would typically be stationed—something that connects with the actuality of situation just mentioned by Vaiśaṃpāyana above (VIII.2.10):

> paśyadhvaṃ ca mahātmānaṃ karṇaṃ vaikartanaṃ yudhi
>
> Look, at the great-souled Karṇa Vaikartana in battle!

Duryodhana—in the poet's voice—now proceeds, for the benefit of his army, to praise Karṇa. As we have observed, the deictic imperative "look!" which the poet exclaims as he describes a far-off scene is more directed at an audience than at his personal interlocutor. Dhṛtarāṣṭra of course is blind.[49] Once again we witness this blurring of voice in the epic which only goes to enhance the vivid quality of that drama. Saṃjaya then, in a few lines, sings of how Karṇa is proclaimed leader, fights, and is felled by Arjuna: so commences the Karṇa *parvan*.

Dhṛtarāṣṭra collapses with grief, realizing that his beloved son Duryodhana

49. Hence perhaps the *ātmanepada*, the 'middle-voiced' form of the verb, implying an act of imagination.

is thus doomed. There are women present, led by Gāndhārī, who are similarly impelled by the grief caused by Saṃjaya's announcement, and they too collapse upon the ground beside the old king. These women, one presumes, are there throughout the song of Saṃjaya, and at this instant 'he animates' or 'consoles' them: *samāśvāsayad* (VIII.3.5).[50]

Saṃjaya opens this Karṇa song with a list of all those Kauravas who have fallen, beginning with Bhīṣma, thus supplying his current poem with a certain dignified formality which coincidently establishes the scene, rather like an overture in an opera (VIII.4.4). The governing term in this long listing of fifty-seven *ślokas* is *hataḥ* 'killed', which is repeated and repeated. Dhṛtarāṣṭra then asks to hear whom among the "sons of Kuntī" have been felled, which Saṃjaya proceeds to tell.[51] It is as if at the commencement of this new *parvan* the poet is analeptically situating the particular song in the sequence of the larger narrative, recapitulating the situation for the audience before the movement of the poetry continues.[52]

Next, Dhṛtarāṣṭra himself assumes the poetic voice and rehearses all of the martial endeavors and abilities of Karṇa, describing his skills and divine weaponry. With this third of the battle books, after the great deeds of combat and duel in the Droṇa *parvan*, it is as if the poets are now recollecting themselves and the state of battle at Kurukṣetra before they engage with the narrative of Karṇa's *aristeia* or 'excellence in battle'. This speech of Dhṛtarāṣṭra's, lasting for one hundred and ten *ślokas*, is almost a micro-epic of its own, singing of all the relevant heroic details that encompassed the mature life of Karṇa.

The old king then makes of his poet an unusual request (VIII.15.1):

> proktas tvayā pūrvam eva pravīro lokaviśrutaḥ
> na tvasya karma saṃgrāme tvayā saṃjaya kīrtitam
>
> Saṃjaya, previously proclaimed by you a champion world-renowned,
> But not by you the famed deeds in battle of one unrenowned.

Dhṛtarāṣṭra asks to hear of such a hero, one who is previously unsung or "unfamed," whose name and deeds have not yet been heard. He wishes to know of *śikṣaṃ prabhāvaṃ vīryaṃ ca pramāṇaṃ darpam eva ca*, his 'skill, splendor, and heroism, authority, and also pride'. The king is in fact asking to hear

50. At VIII.69.41, Gānhdārī is also present beside her husband and collapses senselessly when her husband swoons; this is after Saṃjaya has sung of the death of Karṇa. She is revived by the other women who are present.

51. The word for 'sons of Kuntī' is *kuntayo* rather than *kaunteyā*, an uncommon usage (VIII.4.59). Similarly there occurs the word *kuravas* instead of *kauravās* at VIII.44.2. Such usage appears to be specific to the Karṇa *parvan*.

52. M. C. Smith (1975: 482) notes that VIII.4.90–105 is part of what she terms the "core" epic.

of a hero who has *not* previously entered the song, someone who has *not* yet been mentioned or included in the epic tradition. He is almost testing his poet, making sure that Saṃjaya is not simply drawing upon virtuosity, but ensuring that the song be inventive and innovative, that it be novel.[53] Once again, the audience witnesses a delicate touch by the poets or editors, supplying further vivacity to the performance. This hero is named Pāṇḍya, of whom Saṃjaya proceeds to sing a small epic in itself, describing the champion and then depicting a duel between him and Aśvatthāman at the end of which Pāṇḍya is horribly killed (VIII.15.3–43).

The long descriptions that depict Karṇa as he prepares for his ultimate duel and mounts his chariot I have dealt with elsewhere; they are passages of great beauty and measure and dignify this superlative Indo-European hero as he goes to his much-famed death.[54] Saṃjaya also gives many lines to the seduction and cajoling of Śalya by Duryodhana so that the former will act as charioteer for the superb Karṇa. There is terrific drama and character as well as THEATER in these lines, as the poet subtly interprets his characters as he enacts their words.[55] Karṇa sets out *mṛtyum kṛtvā nivartanam* 'having made death a retreat' (VIII.26.32).

Saṃjaya makes more of this hero's glorious going-out than of any other warrior in the poem, which is significant, and the duel between Karṇa and Arjuna receives more description than any other combat in the epic: this is *the* central moment in the battle books. Either the profoundly mortal Karṇa is the most important hero of the epic Bhārata, as I have argued elsewhere, or Saṃjaya is, in ways that we cannot apprehend, deeply affiliated with the clan or person of this figure.[56] Perhaps in the hypothetical past there existed within the Mahābhārata cycle of poetry an epic that was localized, in the sense that it concerned a geographic area as well as a particular hero, and to that region the clan of Saṃjaya was also affiliated. Such thinking is thoroughly speculative but it does illustrate a possible aetiology for Saṃjaya's great lavishing of poetry upon the song of Karṇa.

As a work of art, among the battle books the Karṇa *parvan* possesses the most accomplishment, integrity, and the most focus, and includes passages

53. Presumed is also the fact that Dhṛtarāṣṭra himself *knows* the tradition otherwise this request would be nugatory.

54. McGrath 2004.

55. I use the word theater here in the sense utilized by Nagy (2009: 1§44 and 1§161). This word conveys the meaning of 'an instrument for seeing'. One can imagine the poet, surrounded by an audience, singing these lines and making the scene distinctly visible for those who surround him. Silent reading, unlike listening, lacks that transferential quality which is induced by the *drama* of the speaker's voice and manner which almost, or ideally, turns an audience into a group of spectators.

56. Karṇa is *the* Sanskrit hero.

that are retrospective and recapitulative for an audience, detailing Karṇa's doings that precede events at Kurukṣetra (VIII.29; 52; 67). As the final duel approaches and the narrative tension increases, Saṃjaya's vocatives to the old king diminish and the narrative becomes more charged and "real" without such pausing shifts of speech. Karṇa is said to possess the 'the body of Death' and is 'difficult to be perceived' (*kālāntakavapuḥ, durnirīkṣyaḥ*), except to Saṃjaya of course (VIII.56.51).

To close this great song of Karṇa, Saṃjaya performs a long monody by Śalya, who is speaking to Duryodhana, intimately describing the carnage of the field and lamenting the demise of the hero (VIII.68). This of course gives voice to the hero whose *parvan* is subsequent.

4. *Śalya* Parvan

Chapter Nine of the Mahābhārata really concerns the last hours and death of Duryodhana rather than the *aristeia* of Śalya. The poetry becomes strange and ghostly, a tone that conduces well to the subsequent Sauptika *parvan*, which is darkly paranormal. As with the three previous books, this *parvan* commences with an interlocution between Vaiśaṃpāyana and his patron Janamejaya. The poet tells of how, after the final collapse of Kaurava forces and Duryodhana's ruin, Saṃjaya returns to the palace at Hāstinapura in a condition of grief and distress. He is said to return *śivirād* 'from the camp', and is described as *bhujāv ucchritya duḥkhitaḥ* 'desperate, arms raised' as he entered the building (IX.1.14–15). 'He wept' (*ruroda*) and tells the king of his son's reputed death. As usual, the *parvan* is begun with a description of what happens at the end of the chapter, and then proceeds to recapitulate the events leading towards that moment, a formality intrinsic to Mahābhārata poetics.

Saṃjaya, 'having entered the city' (*praviśya purīṃ*), has his interview with the king, during which he sings this final battle *parvan*. It is as if his tele-vision and tele-pathy have now become more of a retrospective account of his physical experiences at Kurukṣetra itself. The city, learning from him of the fall of Duryodhana, joins in his grief, *janaḥ sarvaḥ ... praruroda* 'all the people wailed' (IX.1.18). Saṃjaya greets Dhṛtarāṣṭra and lists the newly deceased; only ten men remain out of the vast forces once assembled, and as usual, the old king and his womenfolk all collapse upon the ground, mortified, and the poet himself joins in the weeping. The women are dismissed and Dhṛtarāṣṭra sings a pitiful threnody for his eldest son, addressing him as *mahārāja* and *rājendra*, supreme titles that he himself only possesses. Then in his speech he subtly assumes the voice of Duryodhana, who is addressing himself, the old king and father; roles are reversed and Saṃjaya is the audience of this thoroughly piteous performance, perhaps the most wretched and pathetic moment in the battle books, such is the pathos of this aria (IX.2.9–28). Vaiśaṃpāyana is of course singing these lines.

No one realizes that Duryodhana is only fatally wounded and still survives, although by the end of the Śalya *parvan* this is obvious. Again, there occurs a blurring of narrative for the purposes of emotion and drama, so that the grief can be discharged over a lengthier period. Dhṛtarāṣṭra, regaining his mental equilibrium, asks to hear how this final episode in the war occurred: *akhilaṃ śrotum icchāmi* 'I wish to hear completely', he says (IX.2.65). So begins Saṃjaya's last great performance, which will conclude with his own grief, to such an extent that his magical powers of inspiration fail and depart from him forever.

Saṃjaya commences by reporting what happens on this seventeenth day of conflict, with Duryodhana being spoken to by Kṛpa (IX.3.7ff). Duryodhana responds at length, summarizing his position, his life and *kṣatriya* beliefs and the *ṛṇa* 'debt' that he owes to his fallen heroic peers (IX.4.3–45). Victory for the Pāṇḍavas is, for the Kauravas, *manuṣyadehānāṃ rathanāgāśvasaṃkṣayam* 'the destruction of horses, elephants, and chariots, of the bodies of men' (IX.7.15). The tone or mood of this shortest of the battle *parvans* is terrible and ultimate.

The eponymous Śalya soon falls to a missile of Yudhiṣṭhira's and the burden of this chapter is actually devoted to Duryodhana, his combat and overcoming: one who was once *rathastho rathināṃ varaḥ* 'stood on a chariot, the best of charioteers' (IX.21.1). Saṃjaya says of him—and this is the poet, telling the father of the hero-prince who believes his son to have just perished—how Duryodhana proceeded to that end (IX.21.4):

> yaṃ yaṃ hi samare yodhaṃ prapaśyāmi viśāṃ pate
> sa sa bāṇaiś cito'bhūd vai putreṇa tava bhārata
>
> O lord of the realm, whomsoever warrior I looked at in battle,
> He was piled with arrows by your son, O lord.

Again there is the implication that Saṃjaya is participating in some physical fashion and not simply reporting as he employs his super-vision. He adds (IX.21.7):

> teṣu yodhasahasreṣu tāvakeṣu pareṣu ca
> eko duryodhano hy āsīt pumān iti matir mama
>
> Among those thousand warriors and among yours and the others,
> To my mind there was only one man: Duryodhana!

Indicating his local presence again, Saṃjaya—after a period when the air is so thick with dust that nothing is visible—as it clears he says: *tato'paśyam ... dvaṃdvayuddhāni* 'then I saw the duels [of warriors]' (IX.21.43).

The merging of Saṃjaya's poetry, the song of Jaya, and his accounts of personal participation in the scenes that he relates—so collapsing the inspiration and the actual engagement—culminate when he takes part in the fighting himself (IX.24.46ff). As he now tells of the fray, the *aham* 'I' becomes *vayam* 'we', until Saṃjaya is captured by Sātyaki, having 'fallen insensible upon the earth' (*mūrchitaṃ patitaṃ bhuvi*; IX.24.51). However, the audience hears nothing more of this for a while, as Saṃjaya continues with his narrative of the battle, as if he has forgotten his condition. It is as if he has objectified his own persona and reports upon that individual just as he does for all the other characters; this is a curious disassociation, eerie and weird, and perhaps appropriate for these final scenes in the life of Duryodhana which are all somewhat *unheimlich*.

Then suddenly Saṃjaya quotes Kṛṣṇa speaking to Arjuna, commenting on how "Saṃjaya" had been taken (IX.26.3). Once again, however, he continues to report conversations and situations on the battlefield, and it is as if the confounding of poem and of experience is constantly altering its bias; so that at one point one aspect predominates and at another point it is the other aspect which gives voice. As this is the song of Duryodhana's death being performed before the hero's father, this skewing of poetic subject only adds to the outlandish intensity of the performance. One should recall that at this instant in the epic, of the hundred sons of Dhṛtarāṣṭra only two now remain alive, one of whom is his eldest, the prince Duryodhana.[57] Such is the delicate and careful artistry of these poets and editors, which focuses on the disturbing and deranging aspects of grief to such an extent that the poetics of the song itself become distorted.

Another hundred *ślokas* on, Saṃjaya the captive figure re-appears in the narrative, and is about to be killed by Dhṛṣṭadyumna, who: *udyamya niśitaṃ khaḍgaṃ hantuṃ mām* 'having raised his sharp sword to strike me', is prevented from doing so by the sudden supernatural presence of Vyāsa. The *ur*-poet or first singer commands (IX.28.36):

> mucyatāṃ saṃjayo jīvan na hantavyaḥ kathaṃcana
>
> Release Saṃjaya living! He is in no way to be killed!

There are so many convergent or parallel narratives in these battle books and the problem is—for us as analysts today—not so much to unthread their

57. Sudarśana, the other uterine-brother, is felled at IX.26.48. Yuyutsu is still living, but his mother was only a co-wife of Gāndhārī.

winding but to be able to discern how such imbrication conduces to the vitality and strength of the poetry and its performance. At this instant in the song the concentration of passion and grief are perhaps too unbearable for the poetics to sustain and these self-referential or magical devices are engaged by the poets or editors; there remains no more logic to the narrative, only this merging of emotion and art. The song is beginning to collapse into itself as its sustaining boundaries fail, just as the clan of the Kauravas disintegrates with the demise of Duryodhana and no one remains among the living.

In the next Chapter I examine more carefully this unique relation between Saṃjaya and Duryodhana, poet and hero, as evinced by the Śalya *parvan* and the two subsequent books. Let us now turn to the problem of Saṃjaya's poetics from a more exacting or microscopic point of view and look specifically at his deployment of metaphor.

Saṃjaya's use of metaphor is simply a means for creating systematic affinity within his poetry; it is a way of sustaining the sound of a verse as well as shifting its significance towards another register, embellishing the verse with an attractive quality separate from its ongoing narrative.[58] The battle books of Mahābhārata poetry are completely informed by the semantics of metaphor and this in fact substantiates at least sixty percent of the text. Let us now briefly examine how this works within the versification of Saṃjaya's performance and explore how—under the differing rubrics of sound, vision, and voice—the metaphors at play in these *parvans* galvanize the poem.[59]

Needless to say, the tropes in the poetry are not actually seen nor heard by the poet, they are simply imagined likenesses employed to give tenor and vigor to the song, to vivify its veracity and memorable quality. Also, the similes, metaphors, and metonyms are drawing upon a reservoir of formulae; they are technical mechanisms that are part of the poet's mnemonic system, his word-hoard.[60] Thus when Saṃjaya, describing Arjuna, says: *nṛtyato*

58. Gk. 'carrying from one place to another'; a figure of speech in which one thing is described in terms of another (*OED*).

59. Simile, metaphor, and allegory often merge or blur in their distinction, yet the process is similar: X stands for Y, and meaning is substituted or transferred, as *this* becomes *that*.

60. There is arguably something potentially transcendental in these long formulaic declamations in that their monodic recitative is inducive of a meditative state in the same way that paratactic incantation can establish an altered state of mind. Whatever the deficit of emotion caused by the song, due to the moods of grief, horror, and pity at the violence and destruction of warfare, these repetitive and formulaic verses are potentially soothing and reductive of such deficiency; and in terms of sonority such patternings are arguably *primitive* and leveling. This is certainly the case if one hears a recital of the Mahābhārata today within a temple precinct and listens to episodes taken from the battle books; for the monodic lack of melody is powerful in its fugal and intricate temperament.

rathamārgeṣu ... na kaścit tatra pārthasya dadarśa 'none could see Pārtha dancing in the chariot's track', the dancing itself is like one of these metaphors, as it is subject to the visionary capacity of the poet and to no other perception (VII.64.4).[61] Saṃjaya soon adds to this statement (VII.65.4):

> na tatra kaścit saṃgrāme śaśākārjunam īkṣitum
>
> There in battle, no one was able to look at Arjuna.

It is this inner world of Saṃjaya—visible only to him—which charges his poetry and song with its brilliance and verbal tenacity, and of course, its beauty. It is this *actual* inwardness, the real interiority of voice, that receives so much metaphor; and to such an extent that the battle books are almost *all* metaphor and simile and the narrative merely a small thematic note that is repeatedly sustained and incidentally developed.

Saṃjaya says, describing a duel of Droṇa's, that (VII.30.18):

> tad adbhutam abhūd yuddhaṃ ...
> naiva tasyopamā kācit saṃbhaved iti me matiḥ
>
> That was an amazing fight ...
> To my mind there could be nothing like it.

To say that there is "nothing like something" is to raise its nature even beyond metaphor, or to accept the fact that *only* metaphor can depict such scenes. The word *upamā* is the term in aesthetics to denote the trope of simile; it is something that is measured or of *like* measurement.[62]

Similarly, towards the end Duryodhana's *aristeia*, Saṃjaya says of the combat (IX.22.15):

> na ca nas tādṛśaṃ dṛṣṭaṃ naiva cāpi pariśrutam
>
> Such was neither seen nor heard [before] by us.

Once again the poet dramatizes the uniqueness of the scene: it has no previous reference nor likeness in poetry nor experience and what he observed was never before witnessed. This, on the one hand, emphasizes his magical inspiration, or, on the other hand, gives marvelous credence to what he is describing, and the indistinction between these two aspects of the narrative is highly successful in its nuanced consequence, causing the ambiguity to be *effective* in its reflex of emotion: this is *new* for an audience. Also, if the scene had never before been *heard*, it cannot be part of an oral tradition.

According to the play of metaphor and simile the tactics and duels of the

61. Anuvinda at VII.74.27 is described similarly as *nṛtyann iva* 'as if dancing', as he attacks Kṛṣṇa with a club.

62. From *upa√mā* 'to measure'.

battle, the carnage and the ruin, take on the qualities of the universe at large: sun and moon, stars, light and darkness, hills, seas, lakes and rivers, animals and birds, human rituals, and the elements of matter. All the varieties of cruel combat and its multiform fracas are primarily portrayed by Saṃjaya in terms of the created world and its heaven. Only occasionally are images of pain and agonizing death reported, the misery and distress of war. Saṃjaya employs images to give cosmic beauty and grace to what is essentially violent, brutal, and often revolting. For instance, when arrows are discharged at Arjuna, they strike him in a manner that is glossed by the poet as (VI.98.12):

> te śarāḥ prāpya kaunteyaṃ samastā viviśuḥ prabho
> phalabhāranataṃ yadvat svāduvṛkṣaṃ vihaṃgamāḥ
>
> O lord, those arrows reached the son of Kuntī,
> Entered as birds a lovely fruit-bearing tree.

Agony, pain, the bloody revelation of wounds, all these are colored and patterned with vastly imaginative ease by the poet so that the narrative becomes in fact a great display of wonderfully beautiful and aesthetically abundant if not fertile scenery. The Pāndava army is at one point—when horses run wild with fear—described as being (VI.101.15):

> nipatadbhir mahāvegair haṃsair iva mahatsaraḥ
>
> Like a great lake agitated by the descent of geese.

Whilst, after the fatal wounding of their captain, Bhīṣma, the Kurus are said to be (VII.1.24–25):

> dyaur ivāpetanakṣatrā hīnaṃ kham iva vāyunā
> vipannasasyeva mahī vāk caivāsaṃskṛtā yathā
>
> Like the sky without constellations, like space without wind,
> Like the earth without grain, as imperfect speech ...

Another warrior, Citrasena, is portrayed as (VIII.10.7):

> sa śaraiś citrito rājaṇś citramālyadharo yuvā
> yuvena samaśobhat sa goṣṭhīmadhye svalaṃkṛtaḥ
>
> O king, he—adorned with arrows, a youth amid an assembly,
> Wearing a beautiful wreath, decorated—he shone with youthfulness.

A river runs through these central books of epic Mahābhārata, something that is seen and rarely audible except in its poetry.[63] This *nadī* is arguably

63. Ranero-Antolin (1999) has written specifically on this metaphor. I have also discussed the *nadī* in McGrath 2009: 197–204.

a river of death, but it is also one that, like the original waters which Indra caused to be discharged in Ṛgveda I.32.1–2, brings fecundity into the world. These *āpas* 'waters' began to flow as a primary instant of fertility in the cosmos or 'three worlds', the *triloka*, when Indra secured victory over Vṛtra the *dānava* demon.[64]

There are many systems of metaphor at work in these four books, monsoon clouds and lightning, the sacrificial fire, trees in many forms, the massiveness of mountains, but during these four central battle sections of the epic—and especially the Droṇa *parvan*—the *nadī* receives repeated and uniform mention by Saṃjaya as he describes the combat which he holds within his vision. The term for river in these books is always *nadī,* and not *sarit*, nor *sindhu*, nor *srotas*, all of which words connote 'flowing' or 'running' and the movement of water. *Nadī* bears with it the quality of 'roaring' or 'thundering', the sound of its flooding water.[65] Thus implicit in the use of this word as a simile for battle is the sound of actual physical conflict: a clashing of weapons and the cries of warriors and animals, and it is arguably a foremost metaphor of these central *adhyāyas* of the epic.

The properties of this 'forceful' (*mahāvegā*) river are given in terms of VISUAL qualities rather than in terms of SOUND, and the image first appears in these four books in the fifty-fifth *adhyāya,* where it is glossed as *rudhiravāhinī* 'a flow of blood' moving towards the 'other world', the *paraloka* (VI.55.11).[66] This first lengthy depiction in the battle books occurs when Arjuna is said to cause this flow (VI.55.122–123):

paretanāgāśvaśarīrarodhā narāntramajjābhṛtamāṃsapaṅkā
prabhūtarakṣogaṇabhūtasevitā śiraḥkapālākulakeśaśādvalā
śarīrasaṃghātasahasravāhinī viśīrṇanānākavacormisaṃkulā

Its banks were dead elephants and horses, its mud was flesh filled with marrow and entrails,

64. Vṛtra, 'the encloser' often figured as a serpent: *áhann áhim ánu apás tatarda právakṣáṇā abhinat párvatānām / áhann áhim párvate śiśriyāṇáṃ* 'he killed the serpent, split the sides of the mountains, bored after waters; he killed the serpent lying on the mountain'. The "waters" are considered as divine and feminine, cognate with Avestan *āpō*, and are always given in the plural. They are more fully depicted in RV VII.49.

65. Mayrhofer, s.v. *nad* 'to sound, thunder, roar' (*rauschende, tönende*)

66. The metaphor is transformed and positively amplified by Dhṛtarāṣṭra himself into a vast 'ocean' (*udadhī*) of his own armies, at VI.72.14ff, and at VII.89.11ff; at VII.74.51ff this is a *rathasāgara* 'sea of chariots'. Saṃjaya himself returns to this trope of the *sainyasāgara* 'sea of armies' at VI.74.32; in the same *parvan*, at 79.5, the Kauravas are likened to fluvial Gaṅgā water and the Pāṇḍavas become the ocean and the image re-occurs at VII.89.11ff, and VII.95.2ff. This riverine metaphor is frequently mentioned during the four central books and is explicitly sustained at VI.99.33ff; VII.13.8ff; VII.20.32ff; VII.48.41ff; VII.68.38ff; VII.83.29ff; VII.113.15ff; VII.131.119ff; VII.162.15ff; VIII.36.29ff; VIII.55.38ff; and IX.8.29ff.

> Populous with ghosts and crowds of numerous demons, its grasses confounded with heads, skulls,
> Its current was a thousand bodies, crammed with waves of various shattered breastplates ...

The paraphernalia of battle, the weapons and chariots and banners, are always likened to the marine and mineral life of a river, the crocodiles and fish and other creatures and rocks. All that is attributable to battle becomes a metaphor in this river for the natural and fluvial world, something that is generally rich and harmonious; for rivers in Indian possess a positive valence and are typically and nominally considered as feminine deities.[67]

The *nadī* is partially formulaic, in that the stamp of the metaphor is repeated and re-formed again and again, each time with different elements. As we noted above, this cliché quality is such that in both the Bhīṣma *parvan* and in the following Droṇa *parvan* the trope occurs almost identically, and in both cases this is sung not by the poet but by the old king himself, Dhṛtarāṣṭra (VI.72.14ff and VII.89.11ff).

This river functions like a governing refrain that the poet frequently returns to—particularly during the Droṇa *parvan*—amplifying it and playing with its detail as the audience is constantly reminded of how battle is like this flow where the natural world and the martial world combine and run towards the otherworld. This is one of the key binding metonyms of the song of Jaya. One should recall that the *Indraloka*, which is arguably the site to which the psyche or *ātmā* of heroes proceeds after their death in martial contest, is spatially upwards, whereas this *nadī* of course is naturally going to be flowing downwards into the realm of Death, or Yama.

I propose that the *nadī* is a metaphor of the oral tradition, being a theme upon which the poets—Saṃjaya in the case of the Mahābhārata—can extemporize at will as if in the form of cadenza; like a theme in western symphonic music, it is repeated and operates as a metonym or ornament linking the components of the work, making beautiful the operation of death and warfare.[68] For *kṣatriyas* life derives its valence from participating in this river of blood; the Bhārata war is not simply entertainment for an audience because it bears the elements of moral life, but it is *tattva* 'truth' or reality—for this *kṣatriya* audience—not in a logical sense but in a metaphorical fashion. Listening to the song is creative of or conducive to not only 'merit' (*puṇya*), but I would argue that it actually supplies the audience with an access to this *tattva*, to their social *tattva*. The polysemic metaphor of the *nadī* is central in this poetic system.

67. For Pāṇini at I.4.3 and VII.3.107, the term *nadī* is the sign of feminine words.

68. It is part of a system that creates *montage*. See Grabar 1992 on the various aspects of ornament as "mediation."

In sum, it is these overriding emotions of grief and horror, the pity and outrage—supplied and informed by *unreal* imagery—that are the signatures which allow the poem to remain vital and active in contemporary life in the subcontinent today; it is these emotions that connect the phenomena of the original song to its ongoing manifestation in the twenty-first century. Certainly, the admiration for valor, courage, sacrifice in war, that are so visibly expressed in the epic, are highly pertinent for certain martial groups in present-day India and for their rhetoric.

To make a pertinent addendum here, one uncommon aspect of Saṃjaya's performance occurs in the Droṇa *parvan* where he makes a reference to what we nowadays know as the Rāmāyaṇa; this is when the two *rakṣasas*, Alāyuddha and Ghaṭotkaca, are contending during the night scene. He depicts the combat as being like (VII.153.27):

> harīndrayor yathā rājan vālisugrīvayoḥ purā
>
> O king, as once between Vāli and Sugrīva, monkey-princes.

One realizes that Saṃjaya, as poet, must be familiar with the epic tradition and culture of Rāmāyaṇa in order to make such a comparison; the implication also involves the king, who one can assume must also know of that *other* epic tradition. This gives Saṃjaya great credibility solely as a performer and not just as a *sūta* in the service of a king, to whom he reports and for whom he records the deeds of heroic members of the clan in battle. Implied is another kind of performative tradition and one that is more *mythical* and potentially "more entertaining" and perhaps rhapsodic; it is arguably less immediate, and one where many of the heroes are non-human.[69]

Another subsidiary point of analysis here concerns *not* merely the use and practice of metaphor and metonymy as these occur within the confines of the poem. I accept the definition and usage of these two tropes as given by Jakobson, and it is these two systems of reference, two principles for organizing meaning that—if they are considered as opposing axes—can be seen as constituting a web or fabric of signification within the poem.[70] On the one hand there is the synchronic or systemic, the icon, and on the other hand there exists the paradigmatic or the evolutionary, the index: these are the two hypothetical axes which govern implication.

One can reasonably argue that it is the song of Saṃjaya which supplies

69. Furthermore, Dhṛtarāṣṭra refers to Rāma Dāśarathi himself, at VII.166.12; and at VIII.4.52, Saṃjaya tells of how Ravana was struck down by Rāma.

70. Jakobson 1987: Part I.8; first published in 1956 as *Two Aspects of Language and Two Aspects of Aphasic Disturbances*. Ch.22 was first published in 1965, wherein he discusses the work of C. S. Peirce on the science of signs.

a synchronic element within the overall work of the four central books—because of the way that he and Vyāsa move among the poetry both as characters and as poets—and that the shift from his voice to that of Vaiśaṃpāyana introduces an index or paradigmatic element into the poetry writ large, which is how the central web or tissue is fabricated, or the greater narrative impetus.[71] Saṃjaya's poem, insofar as there exists no definition or statement of time in the language that passes between Dhṛtarāṣṭra and his poet, partakes of more of the nature of the synchronic, whilst the words of Vaiśaṃpāyana are closer to the naturally diachronic. In such a model epic time is not linear but is transversely woven and acquires two dimensions.

Finally, the model of dialogue between the old king Dhṛtarāṣṭra and his poet is never exceeded by Saṃjaya in his performance: there might be three or more speakers involved in a scene, simultaneously on stage, as it were, but the conversation reported is necessarily limited to a series of dialogues.[72] The constraints of performance limit the poets to such measures of diction.[73]

To conclude, Saṃjaya is a poet of great moral and social sensitivity and one whose visual periphery is unlimited, as his vision ranges across the turmoil and horror of Kurukṣetra. Grief is the dominant tone or key of these battle books insofar as the commanding and foremost activity of these books is death. Saṃjaya is the poet of this litany of Jaya, where the victors triumph over death, passing through so much bloody violence with their lives.[74] His is the voice that fits together the song and, to use Nagy's formulation, "he makes visible the song."[75] He merges the song with personal experience, being—as I hope I have shown—both active as performer of the words and as an engaged agent on the battlefield itself. The blurring fusion between these two activities only goes to enhance the drama and vigor of that performance.

71. One should recall that there is no reference to passing time and its governing structure in the dialectic which exists between Saṃjaya and Dhṛtarāṣṭra, whereas Vaiśaṃpāyana is living and speaking long after both these figures have expired.

72. Only once is this paradigm exceeded and then only for a few *ślokas*, when Karṇa and Aśvatthāman argue and have to be mollified by Duryodhana (VII.134.2–6).

73. In the Western operatic tradition, an *aria* is a convergent voice and a *duo* is a divergent voice in song.

74. 'I think jaya clings to the divine', says Karṇa, referring to the supernatural order of destiny: *daivāyattam ahaṃ manye jayaṃ* (VII.133.58).

75. Nagy 2009: 318.

5

Poet and Hero

Duryodhana is a hero whom I would like to focus upon in this chapter as the one especial participant—if not creator—of the war who is in a peculiar counterpoint to the poet Saṃjaya. My text is confined to the two books subsequent to the battle books. One should recall that when Duryodhana is seen to perish by Saṃjaya, the poet's supernatural powers of perception and conception fail him and he becomes ordinarily human once again. Yet as the cynosure of his father's royal attention, Duryodhana had been indirectly the object of much of Saṃjaya's steady critique against the old king's laxity of policy, insofar as he condoned his son's intransigent purpose. At no point does the poet confront the prince and heir-apparent and condemn his policy, however, which is ironic, for he is absolutely consistent and unceasing in his denigration of the son's agency in the war whenever he speaks with the old king, and in fact Saṃjaya usually opens an *adhyāya* with such unfavoring assessment.

As a *sūta*, Saṃjaya is in service with Dhṛtarāṣṭra and he should be reporting on all his sons during the scene of battle. Ideally, he would be standing on the chariot describing the combat to his patron and king. As Duryodhana is the eldest of the hundred sons and heir-apparent—in fact he is the king in practice—he should be receiving great attention during these events at Kurukṣetra.

During the battle books, as the audience has heard, Saṃjaya is active as the poet who performs the song and occasionally participates as a combatant, becoming an agent in the field itself. In the Sauptika *parvan*, he maintains this position only until Duryodhana finally succumbs to his wounds and perishes at the end of the tenth *adhyāya*; thereafter Saṃjaya is essentially only another character in the poem and no longer the source of its movement; his presence in the epic becomes cursory and intermittent for his unworldly mental immanence has deserted him. Once there are no more sons of Dhṛtarāṣṭra in the field or in the narrative Saṃjaya no longer maintains his former poetic skill and becomes merely human again: there is no more inspiration. Then it is that Vaiśaṃpāyana resumes the thread and continues with his own weaving. The Jaya is complete.

As a poet, Saṃjaya began his epic—if one excludes the *ślokas* in the Ādi *parvan* when he listens to Dhṛtarāṣṭra singing his formal and summary lament—with the messenger scenes in the Udyoga *parvan*; the audience perceive Saṃjaya first as a messenger, the *dūta*, and only later as a *sūta*, the poet. He ceases his Sauptika *parvan* narration by closing with the sound of Aśvatthāman lamenting for the death of Duryodhana, who is about to die. There is nothing heavy-handed on the part of the editors of the epic—whoever and wherever and whenever they lived and worked—in how they introduce and then remove this figure of the poet from the song: he enters and his work amplifies, until he is the one who is telling the story, and then he gently recedes from the scene. There is no sudden entry nor unexplained exit, for he is a well-modulated character in the poem, and his arrival and presence in the song are accomplished with great artistry on the part of those hypothetical "editors."

Earlier, in the latter part of the Śalya *parvan*, weaponless, unarmored, and freed, Saṃjaya proceeds towards the city in the evening light of this final day of conflict at Kurukṣetra. On his way he encounters a fatally wounded Duryodhana, the sole survivor of the Kauravas.[1] He tells the old king of this experience (IX.28.40–41):

> ekaṃ duryodhanaṃ rājann apaśyaṃ bhṛśavikṣitam
> sa tu mām aśrupūrṇākṣo nāśaknod abhivīkṣiktum
>
> O king, I saw the solitary extremely wretched Duryodhana.
> He, eyes full of tears, was not able to recognize me.

Both of them remain silent, one preoccupied with grief, the other with pity. So the narrative once more, at this most tense moment—in terms of emotion—becomes less a *rapportage* that is divinely inspired but a personal, terrible, and ghastly account, charging the poetry with its sad force. 'For a moment I was not able to speak', says Saṃjaya (*muhūrtaṃ nāśakaṃ vaktuṃ*; IX.28.42). Then the poet speaks to Duryodhana, telling of his own capture and release and the prince inquires about his brothers and their deaths. Saṃjaya says (IX.28.45):

> tasmai tad aham ācakṣaṃ sarvaṃ pratyakṣadarśivān
>
> To him I told all that I had witnessed.

He adds that only three Kaurava heroes remain living, as Vyāsa had told him. Again, there is a gentle fusion of sources: not inspiration, not experience,

1. Yuyutsu is also alive, but he had crossed the lines before the fighting began and joined with the Pāṇḍavas.

but what he was *told* by Vyāsa. In one line "he sees" and in the following *śloka*, "he hears"; for the song is approaching its end.

Duryodhana requests that the poet tell his father: *brūyaḥ saṃjaya rājānaṃ ... duryodhanas tava sutaḥ praviṣṭo hradam* 'say, Saṃjaya, to the king, Duryodhana your son has entered the lake' (IX.28.49).[2] He asks the poet to speak of him as *suhṛdbhis tādṛśair hīnaḥ putrair bhrātṛbhir eva ca* 'without such friends and also brothers and sons'. One should recall that this is still part of the song and that Saṃjaya is performing before Dhṛtarāṣṭra the grisly pathos and horrible end to his favorite son's life.

Saṃjaya is picked up by the three remaining Kaurava warriors, Kṛpa, Aśvatthāman, and Kṛtavarman.[3] Saṃjaya tells the old king, in direct speech, how they address him and how he informs them of their leader's situation (IX.28.53ff). The three then take him on a chariot to the city—where already women are screaming and lamenting in the town—before they themselves flee into hiding (IX.28.63). All this is related as experience rather than as reported vision: the panic among guards, the terror among city dwellers, all are depicted in the rout. Saṃjaya tells Dhṛtrarāṣṭra of how Yuyutsu—his son but not by Gāndhārī—goes to Yudhiṣṭhira and offers him service (IX.28.75). Vidura too is portrayed, as he returns to the palace. The closing words of this perhaps most emotionally dramatic *adhyāya*—for this marks the genuine moment of defeat—are often told in the present tense, so vivid and immediate are the words; it is as if Saṃjaya is speaking only to the audience and not to Dhṛtrarāṣṭra.

As the battle books approached closure the song of Saṃjaya had reverted increasingly to the speech of formal and sequential narrative; there were no more metaphor-driven combat scenes, for instance. Now, in this *parvan*, the poet—without any verbal display or metaphorical brio—recounts the final hours of Duryodhana, where he is discovered by the Pāṇḍavas and fights a last duel. Curiously, the lake where the hero-prince is hiding submerged is called *Dvaipāyaṇa*. This is the epithet that is uniquely and solely applied to Vyāsa and means 'island-born', as he was born from an isle on the Gaṅgā: the hero has literally returned to his source.[4] There is an internal

2. Homophonous with *hrada* is *hrāda* 'the roar of thunder', *hlāda* 'joy', and *hṛd* 'the heart'. I say this because the final act of Duryodhana is strange and haunting, incomprehensible even on the level of metaphor, and the term *hrada* appears to be inexplicably important in this respect.

3. There is an element of narrative *misdirection* at this point in the Mahābhārata, for the audience has heard of how no Kaurava warriors remain and of how Duryodhana is dead, and yet this is not the case. Again, such artistry only makes for further suspense and drama in the poem, for a superficial fluidity of words to gather force from great depth.

4. Vyāsa, apart from being the originator of the song, is also Duryodhana's paternal grandfather.

self-reflection or self-reference here within the poem, which is enigmatic in its significance (IX.29.53).[5]

Saṃjaya tells the old king of how the sons of Pāṇḍu address the hidden and immersed Duryodhana and of how the latter begs to be allowed to flee alone to a forest; and he says to the victorious Yudhiṣṭhira: 'go, you, O great king, enjoy the earth' (*gaccha tvaṃ bhuṅkṣva rajendra pṛthivīṃ*; IX.30.50). The grave bantering dialogue between the two kings, Duryodhana and Yudhiṣṭhira, continues until the former rises up out of the waters and prepares for his ultimate duel (IX.31.45):

> atiṣṭhata gadāpāṇī rudhireṇa samukṣitaḥ
>
> He rose, club in hand, soaked with blood.

Saṃjaya reverts to his earlier poetic economy or system of metaphors and formulae in order to portray Duryodhana, but the great and intensely powerful recitative of the battle books has departed and the dramatic mood is now different, is more theatrical, as different figures speak and act: all done in Saṃjaya's voice, of course.

He tells of how the deities in the sky applaud at the onset of this duel (IX.54.9), and of how *papāta ... vicitrapuṣpotkaravarṣam uttamam* 'a superb rain of multifarious and lovely flowers descended' from the sky (IX.56.65). The contest takes place and the struggle is soon concluded. Uncommonly, Saṃjaya comments on the advice that Kṛṣna offers, words that bring victory to Bhīma, and he remarks on how this occurs: *dharmacchalam ... śrutvā keśavāt* 'having heard the fraudulent dharma from Keśava' (IX.59.22).[6] Never before in the poem has anyone, and certainly not one of the poets, commented on how Kṛṣṇa manipulates dharma for the benefit of the Pāṇḍavas; this is a remarkable and singular moment in the epic.[7]

Saṃjaya sings his last hymn, proclaiming the valor and victory of Bhīma over Duryodhana in the duel (IX.60.6–16).[8] Then comes a brief farewell aria

5. Perhaps this is a remnant, a fragment like a small potsherd, of what was once a Duryodhana epic, a song that is long lost in time.

6. These words are directed at Bālarāma, the brother of Kṛṣṇa. The former is typically referred to as *sitaprabhaḥ* 'white' as a *niśākara* 'moon' (IX.33.17). This is in literal and metaphorical contrast to his brother who is *kṛṣṇa* 'dark'.

7. Kṛṣṇa himself, as spoken by Saṃjaya, tells of the necessity of his own *upāyā* 'expedience', saying: *na śakyā dharmato hantuṃ* '[they] were not able to strike appropriately', a sentence that he repeats for emphasis (IX.60.57–62).

8. It is notable that during the course of the poem, whenever crisis occurs and events do not run well for a *kṣatriya*, it is *daivam* 'destiny', or literally 'that which comes from the deities', that is always made culpable, and not human endeavor. When the Kauravas achieve their transient victory the claim is that 'by good fortune' (*diṣṭyā*) this has been achieved. There exists a stable counterpoint between these two terms or agencies in the cosmos and the inflection of the words themselves is telling; *jaya* is associated with the word *diṣṭyā*.

by Duryodhana himself—recounted by Saṃjaya, of course—telling of his joy and fortune in all that he achieved; he is expiring without any remorse or anguish for only gladness informs this speech (IX.60.47–50). These moments are followed by divine proclamations, flowers, songs, perfume, all emanating from the sky, as the poet reassures the hero's father of his dying son's moral purity and greatness.[9] All the above is such a strange closing for the war and its last contest, moving away from the turbulent emotions which had previously been dominant.

The scene closes with Saṃjaya saying that Kṛṣṇa set off towards where "the royal son of Ambikā" was, that is, Dhṛtrarāṣṭra, whom the poet now refers to in the third person, as if he is not present, or as if—from the point of view of the audience—he is distancing himself from the narrative (IX.61.38). Then Vaiśaṃpāyana, like a good rhapsode, takes up the song. He tells of how Kṛṣṇa and Dhṛtrarāṣṭra meet and of how Vyāsa was already present yet silent, and he tells of the words given between the old king and his queen and Kṛṣṇa (IX.62.34ff). It is strange that Vyāsa should be party to a scene and yet unspeaking; these last passages that close the war are curiously without firm definition and expected closure and are mysteriously haunting in their indistinction or contrary form.

Once again, however, for now the seams of the narrative are not as smoothly joined as earlier in the poem, Saṃjaya resumes the song. Being—as usual—addressed with a demand by the old king, he speaks in order to depict *further* the terminal hours of Duryodhana. Saṃjaya here puts himself in the place of the interlocutor, for the prince speaks these words directly to him in the vocative: there is a most subtle reversal of speaking.

Duryodhana is lying alone and wounded and sings a long remorseful account of how wrongfully the kingdom was lost despite all his accomplishment and many gifts (IX.63.7–39).[10] The questioning words 'who possesses a better end than me' (*ko nu svantataro mayā*) are repeated severally (IX.63.19ff).[11] The three Sauptika warriors re-appear and Duryodhana again sings of his benign fortunes, repeatedly expressing himself with the term *diṣṭyā* (IX.64.21–29). Thence proceeds the dreadful and gruesome account of the Sauptika *parvan*, which is a coda as it were to the battle books. Saṃjaya tells of how the three last Kaurava warriors set out to unleash havoc and revenge, and as usual, the old king offers his anxious and desperate inquiries in order to cue his poet. The events of this chapter are informed by the

9. David Gitomer's excellent 1992 *JAOS* study of King Duryodhana covers this material well.

10. 'Having seized victory inappropriately', he says (*adharmeṇa jayaṃ labdhvā*; IX.63.14).

11. This cry had been uttered earlier at IX.60.48 and 49.

divine vision of Saṃjaya and not by his personal activity in any moment.[12] It is unique and remarkable how the death of Duryodhana is extended over so much narrative; it is as if time is being gently retarded in the process so that the emotion of grief can be teased out further and further. No other hero is treated in this fashion during his demise.

During the performance of the first half of Book Ten Saṃjaya works as before, his divine vision supplying him with insight into what was occurring during that awful night when battle was finally over and the few survivors slept. Initially he "sees" what happened in the darkness when Aśvatthāman, Kṛpa, and Kṛtavarman crept through a forest: *apaśyanta vanaṃ ghoraṃ*, he says, 'they saw a horrible forest' (X.1.17). It is actually Saṃjaya who is "seeing" this forest, and the audience, hearing his words, in their mind perceive similarly, visually inspired by the voice of the poet so as to apprehend the narrative. Thereafter, when there is a pause in the account and the poet recommences a new *adhyāya*, the verb engaged is usually not concerned with "seeing" but with the fact that someone "heard": *śrutaṃ te vacanaṃ sarvaṃ* 'your speech having been entirely heard', and *kṛpasya vacanaṃ śrutvā* 'having heard the speech of Kṛpa' (X.2.1; and 3.1). It is as if the poet carefully initiates his audience into the narrative by first viewing it but then the sense becomes acoustic as he distances himself from the song.[13]

After a night of awful carnage the three return to their moribund king and tell of the vengeance. Duryodhana is too broken to speak at first but rallies and utters his last words. In the voice of Aśvatthāman, Saṃjaya sings the final lament for Dhṛtarāṣṭra's eldest son, who is about to die, and this is simultaneously his own last performance (X.9.19–45). There is a coda to the lamentation when the voice of Duryodhana himself bids his three companions farewell—and of course, these last words are to be heard by Saṃjaya's solitary audience, the old king Dhṛtarāṣṭra—as Duryodhana becomes 'silent' (*tuṣṇīm*) and finally surrenders his breath. 'We meet again in heaven' is his closing sentence (*svarge naḥ saṃgamaḥ punaḥ*; X.9.53–55). The ending description of him by Saṃjaya is: *vīraḥ suhṛdāṃ śokam ādadhat* 'the hero received the grief of his companions', a gently poetic way to describe the demise of one who—arguably—caused the death of innumerable thousands. Strangely, or rhetorically, Saṃjaya at this point says to the old king (X.9.57):

pratyūṣakāle śokārtaḥ prādhāvaṃ nagaraṃ prati

12. The deity Śiva, in splendid theophany, appears in this *parvan*, from X.6.3 to X.7.63.

13. Unless, that is, he is actually impersonating one of the characters and speaking in the first person. One presumes that the "character plus *uvāca*" stage directions, 'so-and-so said', are editorial inclusions into the text, and did not occur when the preliterate poem was being sung, say, three millennia ago.

Afflicted with grief, at dawn I set out towards the city.

The city being where he is presently, as he speaks with Dhṛtarāṣṭra. This constant shuttering back and forth between immediate past and present supplies the poem with a weird timelessness at this point, as the recumbent and wounded Duryodhana is returned to again and again. Suddenly it is as if the poet was telling of something which occurred in the past, so compressing song and event into one verbal phenomenon, for it is exactly at this moment that his divinely inspired vision deserts him. In the following half of the *śloka* he states (X.9.57):

ṛṣidattaṃ pranaṣṭam tad divyadarśitvam adya vai

That divine sight given by the *ṛṣi* is now vanished.

Thereafter his presence is that of simply another figure in the text and he sings no more epic but only participates in the poem. Immediately, Vaiśaṃpāyana resumes the song.

Saṃjaya continues to be one of the entourage surrounding and supporting Dhṛtarāṣṭra during the scenes depicted by Vaiśaṃpāyana in the next book, Book Eleven.[14] He and the king's half-brother Vidura are constantly there beside the old man as they have been throughout the poem.[15] The mourning scene on the battlefield focuses on Gāndhārī, the single mother of an hundred Kaurava sons; notably, the three Pāṇḍava mothers, Kuntī, Draupadī, and Subhadrā, are not center-stage at this moment.

The opening of the Strī *parvan* has king Janamejaya, the great-grandson of Arjuna—and so the poem is suddenly far removed in time from the battle books—asking his poet: *brūhi yad abhāṣata saṃjayaḥ* 'say, what did Saṃjaya speak?' (XI.1.3). Now that the song of Jaya, the song of Saṃjaya, is concluded, it is the poet Vaiśaṃpāyana who is the one to continue with the strain, and it is as if the poets or editors are fusing the two performances, carefully allowing Saṃjaya to recede without abrupt dismissal. Vaiśaṃpāyana tells of how the *sūta* 'the brilliant one, having approached, spoke the words' *abhigamya mahāprājñaḥ ... vākyam abravīt* (XI.1.5). Saṃjaya is attempting to mollify the old king's vast grief, and advises him (X.1.8):

pitṝṇāṃ putrapautrāṇāṃ jñātīnāṃ suhṛdāṃ tathā
gurūṇāṃ cānupūrvyeṇa pretakāryāṇi kāraya

14. In McGrath 2004 (223), I argued that it is at this point—the end of the Strī *Parvan*—that Epic Mahābhārata closes.

15. At XII.40.6, when Yudhiṣṭhira is being consecrated as Kururāja, Saṃjaya and Dhṛtarāṣṭra are present. Later, the audience hears how Saṃjaya is seen standing on a chariot with Yuyutsu, preceptor to the future king Parikṣit. An important and authoritative figure, Saṃjaya is always at the political center it seems (XII.47.70).

Have performed in order the obsequies of *gurus*,
Of friends, of kin, of sons and grandsons, as of ancestors.

These words of Saṃjaya are overtly given in reported speech by Vaiśaṃpāyana and that manner is not veiled. Of course, it was always the case that this was happening, but not obviously so, as a framing device was in operation. Now it is as if Saṃjaya's speech is given in quotes within Vaiśaṃpāyana's song; this is conversation and injunction by the *sūta*, for his account and *rapportage* are done.

This in fact is what Yudhiṣṭhira later instructs Yuyutsu, Sudharma and Dhaumya (respectively the Kaurava and Pāṇḍava priests), along with Vidura, and Saṃjaya to manage: *ādideśa ... pretakāryāṇi* 'he commanded the obsequies' (XI.26.24–26).

At this point let us recall *what* is actually being spoken—according to the epic's own staging of itself as uttered at the outset of the Ādi *parvan*—in the Naimiṣa forest when Ugraśravas sings of what he heard Vaiśaṃpāyana once saying, and where Vaiśaṃpāyana himself is said to be only retelling what he heard Vyāsa formerly proclaim.[16] The temporal transitions between all these recollections are great—in terms of actual years—and the production of the Mahābhārata, as opposed to the Bhārata, thus encompasses a view of many decades of time. Saṃjaya's song of Jaya is chronologically distinct, and even his words spoken as *dūta* fit with this temporal model: for the song of Jaya is the authentic center of the epic. What the editor-poets have done—in terms of the Mahābhārata—is to establish a location in time for the frame of a very different chronological world. We have seen how the narrative of Saṃjaya often becomes dislocated in a temporal sense, when the poet speaks not from the point of view of inspiration but occasionally of experience. With the voice or presence of Vaiśaṃpāyana this timely situation ranges far more widely, yet these intervening years are blurred by the poetics at work. As I have shown earlier, Saṃjaya is potentially closer to the center of Bhārata events, the battle scenes, than is Vyāsa: for if Vaiśaṃpāyana is merely reduplicating what he had previously *heard* from Vyāsa, then this is logically the case.[17]

16. Remember also that Vyāsa does not offer his song to humanity until all the Pāṇḍavas are deceased; such is another temporal removal of the song from events.

17. Graphically put, the model would be: Ugraśravas > Vaiśaṃpāyana > Vyāsa > Saṃjaya. As I have shown, however, there is a partial occlusion or obfuscation between Vyāsa and Saṃjaya; the artistry of the poet-editors has accomplished this delicate fusion in order to make the poetic seams more unrecognizable. To repeat the observation which I made in the previous chapter at note 69 concerning Jakobson's concepts, it is as if Saṃjaya's poem participates more in the nature of the synchronic whilst the language of Vaiśaṃpāyana is closer to the naturally diachronic. Epic time in such a reading is not a process but a woven fabric that

Saṃjaya's song of victory essentially circulates about the act and the imagery of death, that is his subject and it is death which leads to *jaya*. He sings of how the coalition of Pāṇḍavas, Pañcālas, and Yādavas defeated the assembled Kaurava forces. After all the bloodshed and destruction concludes and annihilation is complete, Kurukṣetra is silent and a place of carrion, scavenging animals, and the sound of women lamenting. Then old king Dhṛtrarāṣṭra is full of misery and remorse for the fatality that encircles him and for the folly of his own judgment in not restraining his eldest son. Victory, *jaya*, has been achieved by the Pāṇḍavas and the old man asks his poet (XI.1.19):

> ko'nyo'sti duḥkhitataro mayā loke pumān iha
>
> What other man is there here on earth more grievous than me?[18]

This is the prompt for Saṃjaya to mourn for the slain, which takes place in the *viśoka parvan*, "the book of the cessation of sorrow" part of the Book of the Women, the Strī *parvan*. His voice is explicitly encapsulated within the speech of Vaiśaṃpāyana now, for no longer does Saṃjaya perform as a poet, having once again become merely the companion of the old king. This dirge is *śokāpaha* 'dispelling of sorrow', and he says: *śokaṃ rājan vyapanuda* 'king, drive off grief!' (XI.1.22). As usual, what he says is critical and full of blame, damning Dhṛtarāṣṭra for his lack of policy and for allowing Duryodhana to wreck the kingdom; even now there is no compassion. During his speech the word "grief," inflected variously, re-occurs forcefully articulated again and again as the poet enjoins the old man to put aside the unhappiness caused by his own delinquency.

Yet instead of conciliating this old man the poet only stresses his weakness and laxity in not doing anything to prevent the calamity which was so obviously due. He in fact blames him for ignoring all the pleas of Bhīṣma, Vidura, and Gāndhārī, and blames the wicked cronies who surrounded Duryodhana and urged him on towards the disaster, Karṇa, Śakuni, and Duḥśāsana. Duryodhana was only interested in 'war' (*yuddham*), and as Dhṛtarāṣṭra did not hinder his son, all the *kṣatriyas* were 'destroyed' (*kṣapitāḥ*; XI.1.26). If only the king had forbidden the dicing in the *sabhā*, he adds, whence all error, cruelty, and death ensued.

Having said this, however, he then turns his message about and instructs the old king: *na tvaṃ śocitum arhasi* 'you do not deserve to grieve' (XI.1.29). Saṃjaya repeats this phrase and variants of it and the noun "grief" five times; anaphora occurs, as we have seen in this epic, when someone is

---

possesses two possible extensions, in which Saṃjaya supplies the *icon* whilst Vaiśaṃpāyana provides the *index*.

18. This of course reverses the dying words of his son: *ko nu svantataro mayā* (IX.63.19).

delivering a specific and precise message, and it is always a ready technique of emphasis. Throughout the epic the audience has constantly listened to Saṃjaya admonishing the king for his equivocation and dilatory manner towards his son, and even at this moment of total dejection, Saṃjaya does not compromise his view, which is surely the intended view of the Mahābhārata itself: the sufficient condition of annihilation was Duryodhana, but certainly, the sole necessary condition lay in the unspoken words of King Dhṛtarāṣṭra. In this message, arguably the TRUTH of the epic, Saṃjaya is the speaker as it is performed. Duryodhana was not restrained, that was the error, and in this it is unkingly and not in good *kṣatriya* form to lament—not the deceased—but for one's own moral ineptitude (XI.1.36).

> jahīha manyuṃ buddhyā vai dhārayātmānam ātmanā
>
> Strike at anger with intelligence! Support the self with the self!

Such are the last and paradoxical words of Saṃjaya in the Jaya epic as such,[19] and such is perhaps the message of the song itself, the purpose lying behind the singing of epic poetry. The song of *Jaya*—through its great artistry and beauty—dispels the anger that is necessarily attached to and connected with the successful or victorious use of violence, which is what *kṣatriyas* do. To employ a term from another but cognate tradition, there exists a possible *KATHARSIS* of grief in the act of listening to epic performance: *dhārayātmānam ātmanā.*

Vyāsa, in his supernatural way, spontaneously appears in order to appease the king, and he is more gentle and uncritical than his substitute, Saṃjaya. His words are spoken by Vaiśaṃpāyana of course, so confounding the distinction—as the audience witnessed with Saṃjaya—between the two selves of poet and character in the narrative.

19. I repeat the assertion here that the epic, the Song of Jaya, closes with the end of the Strī *parvan*.

6

Closure

THE VARIOUS MEMBERS OF THE ROYAL HOUSEHOLD receive their commissions after Yudhiṣṭhira has been consecrated as sovereign in Book Twelve, the Śānti *parvan*, Dhṛtarāṣṭra being entitled to the 'highest divinity' (*daivataṃ param*; XII.41.4). Saṃjaya too, receives his assignment, as the new king determines (XII.41.10):

> kṛtākṛtaparijñāne tathāyavyayacintane
> saṃjayaṃ yojayām āsa ṛddham ṛddhair guṇair yutam[1]
>
> He employed the prosperous Saṃjaya—joined to goodness—with prosperity
> In the perception of what was unaccomplished and accomplished, also in the consideration of receipts and disbursements.[2]

At the end of his life Saṃjaya is described as being still in the company—along with Vidura and Yuyutsu—of the old king; this occurs in the Āśramavāsika *parvan*: he 'attends' (*upātiṣṭhad*) to Dhṛtarāṣṭra, is how Vaiśaṃpāyana says it (XV.1.5). Early on in this book the old king desires to leave the kingdom and to embark upon *vanaprastha* or 'renunciatory life in the forest', and solicits Saṃjaya, requesting that he conciliate Yudhiṣṭhira on this matter so that the latter would allow him to depart (XV.6.19). Saṃjaya acts as instructed but the accomplishment of the request only occurs via the intercession of Vyāsa, who supports the plea; the *ṛṣi* suddenly appeared, as is his manner, and addressed Yudhiṣṭhira (XV.8.22). Once again these two poets merge in their function.

When the old king and his wife Gāndhārī eventually set off towards the forest dressed as renunciants, obviously never to be seen again, the loyal Saṃjaya wishes to remain with his patron. Vaiśaṃpāyana at this instant

1. The word *ṛddha* can also indicate 'filled with voices, made to resound' (Monier Williams). Similarly, *guṇa* can indicate 'the string of a musical instrument'. Both terms thus bear with them this sonorous and musical nuance, appropriately applied to one whose life is that of poetry and singing. In the Vulgate version of the text the word is simply *vṛddha* 'old'. Soon after this moment in the poem Vaiśaṃpāyana gives his fellow poet the epithet *mahādyutiḥ* 'glorious', a rare instance of qualitative recognition (XII.44.14).

2. Perhaps this latter office is something of a sinecure? It does give a pragmatic and official slant to the work and life of this most divine and accomplished poet.

refers to the poet as *mahāmātraḥ*, a term denoting high rank and one that usually indicates what we would consider a 'chief minister' (XV.22.4). Saṃjaya enters the forest in attendance on the king and he dresses in the clothing of a renunciant and fasts and is portrayed as *kṛśo valkalacīravāsāḥ* 'emaciated, dressed in strips of bark' (XV.25.18).

Not long before his own end comes, Dhṛtarāṣṭra is visited by the great *ṛṣi* Nārada, who predicts the future for these mendicants. He does so *divyacakṣuṣā* 'by divine insight', a skill that the audience has heard Saṃjaya to have once been endowed with: that is, the poet in his cosmic ability is likened to this great seer. As we have constantly observed, no other human character in the poem possesses this gift and Saṃjaya is truly exceptional, not simply as a poet but as a mortal being (XV.26.19). Nārada then says of him in the subsequent line that: *svargam avāpsyati* 'he will attain heaven'.

Once, when Yudhiṣṭhira and brothers, in the company of Draupadī, visit the old king and his wife on the shores of the Yamunā river, hordes of forest ascetics come to see the famous ruler and his clan and they request that Saṃjaya, the *sūta*, inform them of the names of all the royal visitors. This is a fine moment of great artistry on behalf of the editor-poets, for what ensues is Saṃjaya's last speech in the Mahābhārata, a song of twelve *triṣṭubh* verses, two-thirds of which depict the Pāṇḍava women (XV.32.5–16). The tone is lyrical, full of simile and metaphor, in which the chief members of the clan and their women are portrayed and aestheticized. Yudhiṣṭhira is a gold-colored lion with prominent nose and large eyes; two other brothers are likened to elephants; the twins are like Viṣṇu and Indra. Draupadī is compared to the goddess Lakṣmī even though he says that she is (XV.32.9):

> madhyaṃ vayaḥ kiṃcid iva spṛśantī
>
> Touching—as it were—middle age.

In the next verse, Arjuna's two other co-wives are there, one like a moon, the other golden; they are followed by the co-wives of the three other brothers and the illustration of women includes the white-clad widows of the sons of Dhṛtarāṣṭra.

This is a beautiful small song, lightly summarizing the senior members of the clan. 'Look', says Saṃjaya (*paśyata*) pointing to them in general before he names and portrays each one individually by the demonstrative *eṣa*, or *eṣā* in the case of the women. This kind of picturing, as we have observed earlier in this epic, is the essential activity which *sūtas* are specialized in performing.[3] As this song stands as the conclusive performance of Saṃjaya, it is

3. See above, Chapter Two.

as if the editors or early poets were giving him one final and sovereign moment on the stage and there is an air of valediction to his words. Looking back almost, he praises the beauty of those characters who have figured in his song and the governing emotion is grief.[4]

The last mention of Saṃjaya in the poem occurs when the old king finally perishes in a forest fire. Immediately prior to that, the poet is said to be (XV.45.17):

> saṃjayo nṛpater netā sameṣu viṣameṣu ca
>
> Saṃjaya is the leader of the king in the rough and the plain.

Netā is an ancient and loaded term, indicating the conductor or one who guides; Saṃjaya, as we have observed, is the one who has also conducted and led the song of Jaya.

Near the Gaṅgā one day the trees catch fire and threaten all life. Dhṛtarāṣṭra, knowing that death is imminent, instructs his poet to depart and escape the flames: *gacccha saṃjaya*, he says, 'Go'. Saṃjaya, aware that the fire is deathly, anxiously replies (XV.45.25):

> na copāyaṃ prapaśyāmi mokṣaṇe jātavedasaḥ
>
> I do not *see* a means of escape from the fire.

Even at the last, Saṃjaya is one who thinks visually, sight being his primary medium in life.

The king, accepting death, repeats his injunction to the poet, *gaccha*, and accompanied by Gāndhārī and Kuntī settles down to wait, facing the east. Saṃjaya circumambulates the trio and speaks his last words in the Mahābhārata to the old king, directing him (XV.45.29):

> uvāca cainaṃ medhāvī yuṅkṣvātmānam ...
>
> The wise one said to him, 'Yoke your self'.[5]

Vaiśaṃpāyana comments a few lines after this that the poet, here described as a *mahāmātras* 'chief minister', managed to flee the conflagration and that Vaiśaṃpāyana himself once observed Saṃjaya on the shore of the Gaṅgā surrounded by ascetics.[6] Finally he is described as (XV.45.33):

4. M. C. Smith (1992: 156) considers these lines to be part of the oldest core of the epic.

5. Or, 'yoke your mind'. It is indicative of the poetic sharpness and precision of those early editors and poets that the final words of Saṃjaya in both the Bhārata and the Mahābhārata are almost identical injunctions concerning *ātma* the 'self': at XI.1.36 given above, and here at XV.45.29. Similarly, when Saṃjaya makes his initial entry into the poem at I.1.95, he is said to be *medhāvī*; at that point it is Ugraśravas who is speaking for Vaiśaṃpāyana had not yet appeared.

6. If that was actually the case, Saṃjaya must have been very old and Vaiśaṃpāyana very young!

prayayau saṃjayaḥ sūto himavantaṃ mahīdharam

Saṃjaya the poet set off towards the mountainous Himālaya.

Thus the Bhārata poet does not actually die but continues on towards a region of India that is traditionally considered eternal in its ways: so his immortality is hinted at by Vaiśaṃpāyana.

To conclude now on another note of metaphor, during the long peroration that Bhīṣma speaks as he lies recumbent upon a deathbed of arrows, Vaiśaṃpāyana describes a moment in this scene, depicting those who surround the dying hero. He makes use of an unusual and unique image (XIII.166.4):

abhūn muhūrtaṃ stimitaṃ sarvaṃ tad rājamaṇḍalam
tūṣṇīṃ bhūte tatas tasmin paṭe citram ivārpitam[7]

All that circle of kings became momentarily calm,
Like a painted sketch—become silent then—in that picture.

These two lines from the Anuśāsana *parvan* illustrate what would appear to be a unique point. The poet is not referring to a situation of divine vision of the deities or heroes to which he has unique and privileged access, but he calls upon a picture, a visible artifact: he is describing not divinity nor natural reality but another work of art, something already described in another and human medium. This is the group of kings assembled about a dying figure, taken from a shrine, a fresco, a tapestry or weaving, or even a 'painting' as such (*citra*). A thing has interposed itself between object and speech and there is a marked shift from nature, including divine nature, to a world of *likeness* that is in itself poetic metaphor.[8] In terms of ancient literary criticism, the values of those early editor-poets have moved from a condition of multiformity of text to a situation where, in terms of metaphor, there is a new moment that is *static*.[9]

The circle of kings, of course, refers not only to the *citra* but also to the group of Pāṇḍavas who ring the supine Bhīṣma; it is as if Bhīṣma is projecting

7. This *śloka* occurs in the Vulgate edition of the text and only the second line of it exists in the CE, at XIII.152.1 as: *tūṣṇīṃ bhūte tadā bhiṣme paṭe citram ivārpitam* 'When Bhīṣma became silent, like a painted sketch on a cloth'. The variant reading below the line, 714*, is given.

8. A similar moment occurs in the Homeric Iliad in Scroll XVIII with the Shield of Achilles and also in scroll III.125, where Helen is described as weaving a *mègan històn*, a 'great web', whereupon she depicts the battlefield scenes. J. D. Smith (1991: 64–65) writes of the *par*, a 'story-cloth' that contemporary epic singers utilize in Rajasthan.

9. There are several other moments in the poem that are mildly similar to this, when the embellishment of weapons or the images on the *dvajas* or banners are given, but they are always in passing and never receive the visual force that this picture possesses, for those images do not depict human beings.

himself into the *picture*, and the implication of this metaphor is that the epic itself is *citra*, and that the epic poem is something *pictured*.

An even more graphic moment of ekphrasis occurs early on during the Bhīṣma *parvan* when Saṃjaya is describing to the old king how the battle at Kurukṣetra commences, where Bhīma is the first assailant to be described in particular. As the clash begins, the poet says (VI.42.25):

> kurupāṇḍavasene te hastyaśvarathasaṃkule
> suśubhāte raṇe'tīva paṭe citragate iva
>
> Both Pāṇḍava and Kuru armies, crammed with chariots, horses, elephants,
> Shone in battle like a picture on a cloth.

Again, Saṃjaya is making a rare shift from the natural world to that of artifice or artistry. It is tantalizing to wonder what this *paṭa* was and what service such objects performed in palaces, camps, households, or perhaps even poetry, as either woven, embroidered, or pigmented; for here is depicted a unique scene of battle itself—but not in words—yet it is exactly the same object as Saṃjaya is portraying in his speech. He is *creating* a picture with his song yet suddenly the axis of representation has shifted.

The origins of criticism always begin with a *description* of the work of art, an activity where the values of judgment are engaged by the scholiast: that is the foundation for critical activity, and Saṃjaya is here performing, albeit momentarily and summarily in compressed form, that critical act. This kind of distinction between those who bear the poem and those who are trained critics occurs right at the onset of the work (I.1.51):

> vyākhyātuṃ kuśalāḥ kecid granthaṃ dhārayitum pare
>
> Some [poets-*vipras*] are skilled in exposition, other bear the composition.[10]

Nīlakaṇṭha would be a later figure in the former class as would Sukthankar; whereas Saṃjaya is one of the latter group. It is noteworthy that even early on in the life of the epic there existed a tradition of critique, and, one presumes this marks the commencement of an editorial tradition.[11] Sukthankar's disdain for the Vulgate editors' lack of critical regard in their objectivity of

10. The word *vipra* can mean 'poet, wise one, brahmin'. The word *grantha* implies that which has been strung or bound together, either a narrative or later, a physical object itself.

11. Certainly, Nīlakaṇṭha was primarily a commentator and Sukthankar primarily an editor and their material differs in production, yet both worked in critical traditions or systems of literary judgment which drew upon highly distinct critical values. Both assembled textual variants in their effort to arrive at a more *certain* text of the poem, or a more precise poetic *truth*.

textual selection is based upon his view that their critical technique was idiosyncratic and unmethodical: merely fitting words together inventively and autonomously in order to activate the poem according to their views.[12] Poetic licence often dominated this conception of the poem and one can easily imagine such editors "fixing" the text, inserting *ślokas* of their own design and creation in order to secure a more wholesome version of the poem that was in accord with their understanding of how it tallied with dogmatic or spiritual beliefs. All such materials were athetized by Sukthankar in his Critical Edition.[13]

At the very end of the epic as we have it in the Critical Edition today, there comes the line (XVIII.5.39):

> jayo nāmetihāso'yaṃ śrotavyo bhūtim icchatā
>
> Victory is the name of this story; it is to be heard by one desiring fortune.[14]

For *kṣatriyas* whose ambition is rule and domination, there is only one sign in their world that will sustain such a desire, and that is JAYA; a king or hero or warrior in order to succeed in these offices must be triumphant. This also applies to the veracity of legal or political speech, that is law-giving, as well as to the activities of courage and violence and to loyalties inherent in hierarchy.

As with Bhīṣma and Droṇa, Saṃjaya is in a position of dilemma in the Kaurava court or household: for he is bound by loyalty and hierarchy and yet it is obvious to him and others that Duryodhana is behaving in a manner that does not subscribe to the proprieties of correct princely dharma. As a poet, however, he is bound to record verbally what it is that he perceives, and in particular—as we have seen—this concerns what he sees. The perception of moral dilemma and yet the necessity of action as well as the cosmic inefficacy of mortal action, lies at the heart and core of what the epic teaches; and in this respect, 'victory' (*jaya*) is a mark of *moral* success, a consequence of right action within the 'universe', the *triloka*.[15] It is the purpose of

12. "For the text of the Vulgate is so corrupted and so obviously contaminated that it would be a criminal neglect of duty for any intelligent editor now to reprint the Vulgate, when he has at hand the material to control its vagaries and to correct its absurdities" (Sukthankar 1944: 106).

13. Sukthankar (1944: 101) wrote that, "Nīlakaṇtha has disfigured his text." Sukthankar treated the text as a frozen object, not as an ongoing living component of Hindu culture and society.

14. Victory is also where the epic commenced: *jayam udīrayet* (I.1.0).

15. One should recall that dharma will *always* be imperfect insofar as during the *kali yuga* perfection is only possible in part.

this book to demonstrate that Saṃjaya, as the central poet in the epic narrative, distributes the words that depict in detail—for *kṣatriyas*—how this happens.[16]

Jaya or victory in epic Mahābhārata is the key to the poem's narrative force, this is what is at stake for the heroes, and for the poet Saṃjaya, this is the process which he depicts in his song and with metaphor. For Saṃjaya, the conflict which he portrays is *directly* visible to his viewing: what he *says* is almost always what he *sees* and he is thus able to supply veracity to *kṣatriya* culture in the song.[17] Just as in the act of ekphrasis a poet is distanced from the scene described by the imposition of another artificer, so in the singing of the epic Mahābhārata the victory song of Saṃjaya is removed from the exacting truthfulness of Vaiśaṃpāyana's performance: the sense is different, in that sound rather than vision is at work, but the act of disjunction is homologous. *Jaya* is in this sense—for Vaiśaṃpāyana—fixed and static, for it is something that he has finitely heard; this is just as the *citra* of the above image—or the Shield of Achilles—is also motionless in fact.[18] Vaiśaṃpāyana repeats this exactly, whereas Saṃjaya interprets what he sees; Vaiśaṃpāyana is reporting Saṃjaya's work of art.

On the temporal level, as we have noted, Vaiśaṃpāyana is far removed and distant from the physical being of this other poet, whose song occurred many years earlier and which he has *heard* as a fixed and static acoustic object; whereas Saṃjaya's song concerns the immediate and mutable. Arguably, it is the unchanging, the motionless which is ultimately the nature of the truthful, for that fixed quality, rather like a gold standard, is not fungible but in fact generates standards for all other value. Worth, ultimately, should always approximate to something akin to a Platonic type if it is to be in any way generative of standards.

Jaya as a single word is an imperative form meaning: 'conquer!' or 'win, succeed!' The many tens of hours which were necessitated in terms of an audience's attention, if they were to attend a performance of the battle books, would communicate this inspiring or imperative message. Having sat through many hours of performance—at remote shrines and in small villages in the desert of western Gujarat—I can testify to how intoxicating and haunting these recitals can be, continuing from dusk into the late night, as

16. Davis (2010: 1–3), writing about dharma, says that, "Law is the theology of ordinary life", and, "Theology is the attempt to understand or to give meaning to the transcendent significance of acts."

17. To see and to know are intricately involved as verbs, going back to IE *weid. As I have shown, Saṃjaya is the one poet who certainly *knows* what is happening at Kurukṣetra; a knowledge transmitted down through millennia as *veda* and accepted as such even in the twenty-first century subcontinent.

18. The image reported by an act of ekphrasis is of course not only static but necessarily silent. The "Ode On A Grecian Urn," by John Keats, plays with this *silence*.

the song takes on vivid and almost supernatural qualities during the unlit darkness. Personally, these are the times when I have felt closest to the ancient and ghostly figures of India and its original and *ideal* forms, their forces and powers; for it was as if the song was actually and efficiently invoking such ancient otherworldly and heroic beings.[19]

As it has been stated in the Ādi *parvan*, Vyāsa only performed the epic song in the human world once the Pāṇḍavas were no longer living; implied here is the corollary death of the poet Saṃjaya, for Vyāsa only created the song once all the combatants were no more alive (I.1.56). As Bruce Sullivan has shown, Vyāsa manifests the semi-mortal presence of the sovereign deity Brahma on earth, he is that earthly ritual substitute.[20] Saṃjaya, given his all-encompassing supra-human consciousness is fully allied with that absolute mind of Vyāsa, for, as we have observed, he is just as omniscient as Vyāsa is.[21] The latter focuses more in his discourse or awareness on what we would call *myth* or the fabulous antecedent time of the story, whereas Saṃjaya's discourse is more directed at the *historicity*, the immediate qualities of the Bhārata war. It is a nice conceit on the part of the poets or editors for Saṃjaya to be—in terms of the poem—dead when the song occurs in the Naimiṣa forest, and a paradox, for he is so profoundly and completely vivifying, more than any other figure in the poem. This is in terms of his speech which provides life and dramatic modulation to so many characters in what is essentially the epic centrality of the Mahābhārata.[22]

It is ironic that Saṃjaya, *unlike* any other active character in the epic, has no kinship relations whatsoever apart from receiving a patronym indicating male parentage.[23] It is as if he contains so much within him that kinship

19. I have been fortunate to attend many and various *kṣatriya* rituals and ceremonies in the Kacch of western Gujarat, and my gratitude is due to his Highness the Mahārao of Kacch, Pragmulji III.

20. Sullivan 1990.

21. He does lack the ability to appear and disappear at will, however, although even this is blurred and uncertain.

22. The name of this forest, the Naimiṣa, derives from *ni miṣ* 'to shut the eyes, to wink'. This is an ironic title for the forest as so much poetry, in varying dimensions, is witnessed there. Hiltebeitel has written on this name (2001: 92ff).

23. Perhaps one can remark that just as Vyāsa enters the poem and departs at will, so too does Saṃjaya enter the battle and depart at will. On one hand, it is the immediate lineage of Vyāsa that supplies the central substance of kinship in the poem, whilst conversely, Saṃjaya is one of the uncommonly few figures in the epic to possess no kinship relations at all. There thus exists a great symmetry or *twinning* between these two seeing-poets. The idea of twins as an Indo-European trope has been finely studied by Frame (2009: Part 2); and Nagy (1979: 292–293), has looked at the phenomenon of the *therapōn* or 'ritual substitute' as it concerns Achilles and Patroklos. In McGrath 2004 (Chapter Three), I have analyzed the idea of the equivalent nature that occurs between heroic figures: Karṇa and Duryodhana, Arjuna and Kṛṣṇa, and

and human affinity, apart from the emotional intimacy that he maintains with the old king, is irrelevant and unnecessary. He is also one of a mere handful of survivors of the terrific war, one of the very few who were alive at the outset of the poem: something else that also sets him apart and distinguishes him for his high moral authority.

Perhaps it is worth noting that the first poet of whom the audience hears is described as *sauti*, 'the son of a *sūta*', and that is of course Ugraśravas. In terms of the profession of poetry only Saṃjaya is described as a *sūta* and so in terms of either coincidence or of metonymy, these two figures are thus linguistically connected.[24] The intentionality and determinacy of the Mahābhārata poets, as I hope to have shown in this study, is never casual nor random and the details of performance are always precise and right, however lightly spoken.[25]

I would like to believe, and I hope that I have led the reader in this direction even if I have not managed to convince him or her of the fact, that the song of Jaya in epic Mahābhārata—a song of horses, of elephants, and of heroes—is performed by the eponymous Saṃjaya in a luminous, radiant, and super-conscious fashion: he is the true self, the *ātmā* of the epic poem, not Vyāsa. Made manifest and demonstrated by that song is the dharma, the ethical code of warrior and ruler conduct which lies at the heart of all *kṣatriya* life two if not three millennia ago.[26] Thus when the poet sings *yato dharmas tato jayaḥ* he is making explicit during his performance of the JAYA song all that is dharmically *right* and proper for heroes and kings and the epic is a mimesis of that

Bhīṣma and Rāma, as well as studying the *bhāga*, the symmetrical 'opponent' of combat. The idea of a conjoint figure in epic narrative is well attested and ancient in its provenance and the binary quality of two characters, particularly in terms of life and death, is well founded in this poetry where crucial figures participate in a function of *doubleness*.

24. In Indo-Iranian antiquity poets were traditionally always part of a lineage or clan: that was the nature of their assembly and primary social condition. Even today in western India the profession of bardic poetry is lineal and familial. To make a connection between Ugraśravas and Saṃjaya based upon the use of a single term is thus not too extreme. There exists the Western example of the clan of the Homēridai in Greece.

25. Close reading or *explication de texte*, is what I would describe as *critical pattern making*.

26. Olivelle (2009: 1) writes that "The presenting of Yudhiṣṭhira and Rāma as *dharmarājas* can be seen ... as deliberate challenges to the other king of *dharma*, the Buddha, whose *stūpas* ascribed to Aśoka are significantly called *dharmarājikā*." That the large text of the Mahābhārata as we have it now came from a redaction made in political response to the Aśokan reforms seems likely, athough there is little actual substance in the poem to support this opinion; see Hiltebeitel 2005. Olivelle does cite, however, III.188.64–68, *eḍūkān pūjayiṣyanti* 'they will worship *stūpas*', as likely evidence. *Eḍūka* is a term indicating a bone-house; the word *caitya* 'funeral mound or hall' is also mentioned in these verses (Olivelle 2009: 3). What I have been arguing concerning the Jaya narrative would thus relate to poetry that was extant—in its origins—prior to the reign of Aśoka; one would exclude the Gītā from this view.

vision.[27] This instant also serves us as a point of departure or fountain for modern humanism.

27. The future of Mahābhārata studies perhaps lies in an analysis of how early commentators, editors, and poets achieved the arrangements of the text which we have received: what were the principles and critical values with which they worked? Sukthankar (1944: 263–276) has summarized the scholia, and this marks a beginning for further research into an unmapped area.

Bibliography

Allen, N. J. (2000), *Categories and Classifications*, New York.

—— (2009a), "L'Odysée comme amalgame: Ulysse en Ithaque et comparaisons sanscrites," *Gaia* 12: 79–102.

—— (2009b), "Iliad and Mahābhārata: the Quarrel among the Victors," in: F. Delpech and M. V. Garcia Quintela (eds.), *Vingt ans après George Dumézil (1898–1986)*, Budapest, 271–284.

—— (2010), *Homer-Mahābhārata Comparison: Heroes and Functions*. Unpublished paper, Fourth Annual International Conference on Comparative Mythology, Harvard University.

Aristotle *Poetics*, *see* Halliwell 1995.

Austin, J. L. (1962), *How to Do Things with Words*, Cambridge, Mass.

Bakker, E. J. (1993), "Discourse and Performance: Involvement, Visualization and Presence in Homeric Poetry," *Classical Antiquity* 12: 1–29.

—— (1997), *Poetry in Speech*, Ithaca.

Beissinger, Margaret H. (1999), *Epic Traditions in the Contemporary World*, Berkeley.

Bigger, Andreas (1998), *Balarāma im Mahābhārata*, Beiträge zur Indologie, vol. 30, Wiesbaden.

Bhattacarya, Pradip (2009), "Review of *Stri: Women in Epic Mahabharata*," at: www.boloji.com/bookreviews/187.html.

Bowles, Adam (2007), *Dharma, Disorder, and the Political in Ancient India*, Leiden.

Brockington, John and Mary Brockington, trans. (2006), *Rāma the Steadfast*, London.

Brockington, M. and P. Schreiner, eds. (1999), *Composing a Tradition: Concepts, Techniques and Relationships*, Zagreb.

Burgess, Jonathan S. (2009), *The Death and Afterlife of Achilles*, Baltimore.

Calame, C. et R. Chartier (2004), *L'identités d'auteur dans l'antiquité et la tradition europėene*, Grenoble.

Chakrabarti, D. K. (1992), *The Archaeology of Ancient Indian Cities*, Delhi.

Chadwick, N. K. and V. Zhirmunsky (1969), *Oral Epics of Central Asia*, Cambridge.

Das, Gurcharan (2009), *The Difficulty of Being Good*, Delhi.

Davidson, O. M. (1998), "The Text Of Ferdowsī's Shāhnāma and the Burden of the Past," *Journal of the American Oriental Society* 118: 63–68.

Davis, Donald R. Jr. (2010), *The Spirit of Hindu Law*, Cambridge.

Dumont, Louis (1983), *Affinity as Value*, Chicago.
Elmer, David F. (2005), "Helen Epigrammatopoios," *Classical Antiquity* 24.1: 1–39.
Evelyn-White, Hugh G., ed. (1914), *Hesiod, Homeric, Hymns, and Homerica*, Cambridge.
Finkelberg, Margalit (2005), *Greeks and Pre-Greeks*, Cambridge.
Fitzgerald, James (2004), *The Book of the Women. The Book of Peace, Part One*, Chicago.
—— (2006), "Negotiating the Shape of Scripture," in: Patrick Olivelle (ed.), *Between the Empires*, New York, 257–286.
Foley, J., ed. (2005), *The Blackwell Companion to Ancient Epic*, Oxford.
Ford, A. (2002), *The Origins of Criticism*, Princeton.
Fortson, Benjamin W. (2004), *Indo-European Language and Culture*, Oxford.
Frame, Douglas (2009), *Hippota Nestor*, Washington.
Gitomer, David L. (1992), "King Duryodhana. The Mahābhārata Discourse of King and Virtue in Epic and Drama," *Journal of the American Oriental Society* 112.2: 222–232.
Gode, P. K. (1942), "Nilakaṇṭha Caturdhara, The Commentator of the Mahābhārata," *Annals of the Bhandarkar Oriental Research Institute* 23: 146–161.
Goldman, Robert and Muneo Tokunaga, eds. (2009), *Epic Undertakings*, New Delhi.
Grabar, Oleg (1992), *The Mediation of Ornament*, Princeton.
Guha, Ranajit (2002), *History at the Limit of World-History*, New York.
Halliwell, Stephen, ed. (1995), Aristotle *Poetics*, Cambridge.
Hesiod, *see* Evelyn-White 1914.
Hiltebeitel, A. (2000), *Rethinking India's Oral and Classical Epics*, Chicago.
—— (2001), *Rethinking the Mahābhārata*, Chicago.
—— (2005), "Buddhism and the Mahābhārata," in: Federico Squarcini (ed.), *Boundaries, Dynamics, and Construction of Traditions in South Asia*, Florence, 107–131.
—— (2006), "The Nārāyaṇīya and the Early Reading Communities of the Mahābhārata" in: Patrick Olivelle (ed.), *Between the Empires*, New York, 227–255.
—— (2010), *Dharma*, Honolulu.
Holtzmann, A. (1892–95), *Das Mahābhārata und seine Teile*, 4 vols., Kiel.
Honko, Lauri., ed. (2000), *Textualization of Oral Epics*, Berlin.
Hopkins, E. Washburn (1888), "The Social and Military Position of the Ruling Caste in Ancient India," *Journal of the American Oriental Society* 13: 57–372.
Horsch, Paul (1966), *Die Vedische Gathā und Śloka Literatur*, Bern.

Jakobson, Roman (1981), *Essais de linguistique générale*, Paris.
—— (1987), *Language in Literature*, ed. Krystyna Pomorska and Stephen Rudy, Cambridge, Mass..
—— (1990), *On Language*, ed. Linda R. Waugh and Monique Monville-Burston, Cambridge, Mass.
Jamison, Stephanie (1994), "Draupadi on the Walls of Troy" *Classical Antiquity* 13.1: 5–16.
—— (2007), *The Rig Veda between Two Worlds*. Collège de France, Publications de l'Institut de Civilisation Indienne, série in 8, fascicule 74, Paris.
de Jong, J. W. (1975), "Recent Russian Publications on the Indian Epic," *Adyar Library Bulletin* 39: 1–42.
—— (1985, 1986), *The Study of the Mahābhārata*, Parts I and II, Tokyo.
Kinjawadekar, Pandit, ed. (1979), *Mahābhāratam*, with commentary of Nīlakaṇṭha, 6 vols., New Delhi.
Kinsella, Thomas, trans. (1970) *The Tain*, Oxford.
Koch, John T. and John Carey (2003), *The Celtic Heroic Age*, Aberystwyth.
Kurke, Leslie (1991), *The Traffic in Praise*, Ithaca.
Kuznetsova, Irina (2007), *Dharma in Ancient Indian Thought*, Kilkerran.
Lessing, Gotthold Ephraim (1766), *Laokoon, ober Über die Grenzen der Mahlerey und Poesie*, trans. Ellen Frothingham (1898), Boston.
Lord, A. B. (1960), *The Singer of Tales*, Cambridge, Mass.
Mankekar, Purnima (1999), *Screening Culture*, Durham.
Mani, Vettam (1964), *A Purāṇic Encyclopaedia*, repr. 1975, Delhi.
Mahābhārata, see Sukthankar (1959).
McGrath, Kevin (2004), *The Sanskrit Hero: Karṇa in Epic Mahābhārata*, Leiden.
—— (2009), *Strī: Women in Epic Mahābhārata*, Boston.
McHugh, James Andrew (2008), *Sandalwood and Carrion: Smell in South Asian Culture and Religion*, Ph.D. dissertation, Harvard University.
Mayrhofer, Manfred (1956), *Kurzgefaßtes etymologisches Wörterbuch des Altindischen*. 3 vols., Heidelberg.
Miller, Dean A. (2000), *The Epic Hero*, Baltimore.
Minkowski, Christopher (2005), "What Makes a Work Traditional? On the Success of Nīlakaṇṭha's Mahābhārata Commentary," in: Federico Squarcini (ed.), *Boundaries, Dynamics, and Construction of Traditions in South Asia*, Florence, 225–252.
Mishra, Mahendra Kumar (2007), *Oral Epics of Kalahandi*, Chennai.
Moulton, C. (1974), *Similes in the Homeric Poems*, Göttingen.
Nagy, Gregory (1979), *The Best Of The Achaeans*, Baltimore.
—— (1990), *Pindar's Homer*, Baltimore.
—— (1996a), *Poetry as Performance*, Cambridge.
—— (1996b), *Homeric Questions*, Austin.

—— (2000), "Dream of a Shade: Refractions of Epic Vision," *Harvard Studies in Classical Philology* 100: 97–118.
—— (2003), *Homeric Responses*, Austin.
—— (2004b), "Transmission of Archaic Greek Sympotic Songs: From Lesbos to Alexandria" *Critical Inquiry* 31: 26–48.
—— (2009), *Homer the Classic*, Washington.
—— (2010), *Homer the Preclassic*, Berkeley.
Olivelle, Patrick, ed. (2006), *Between the Empires*, New York.
—— (2009), *Aśoka*, Delhi.
Pargiter, F. E. (1908), "The Nations of India at the Battle between the Pāñèus and the Kauravas," *Journal of the Royal Asiatic Society* 1908.1: 309–336.
—— (1913), *The Purāṇa Text of the Dynasties of the Kali Age*, Oxford.
—— (1922), *The Ancient Indian Historical Tradition*, London.
—— (1938), *Dynasties of the Kali Age*, Delhi.
Parry, M. (1932), "Studies in the Epic Technique of Oral Versemaking," *Harvard Studies In Classical Philology* 43: 1–50.
Parsons, Talcott (1967), *Sociological Theory and Modern Society*, New York.
Pathak, Shubha (2006), "Why Do Displaced Kings Become Poets in the Sanskrit Epics?" *International Journal of Hindu Studies* 10.2: 127–149.
Pattanaik, Devdutt (2008), *The Book of Ram*, New Delhi.
Printz, Wilhelm (1910), "Bhāsawörter in Nīlakaṇṭha's Bhāratabhāvadīpa und in anderen Sanskritkommentaren," *Zeitschrift fur vergleichende Sprachforschung* 44: 69–109.
Ranero-Antolin, Anna Maria (1999), *Similes in the Mahābhārata*, Ph.D. dissertation, Harvard University.
Reichl, K., ed. (2000), *The Oral Epic: Performance and Music*, Berlin.
Renfrew, Colin (2008), *Prehistory*, London.
Rocher, Ludo (1958), "The Ambassador in Ancient India," in: *Indian Year Book of International Affairs*, Madras, 7:344–360.
Rohde, Erwin (1898), *Psyche: Seelencult und Unsterblichkeitsglaube der Griechen*, Freiburg.
Rousseau, J.-J. (1755), *Essai sur l'origine des langues*, repr. 1967, Paris.
Salomon, Richard (1995), "On Drawing Socio-linguistic Distinctions in Old Indo-Aryan: The Question of Kṣatriya Sanskrit and Related Problems," in: Georg Erdosy (ed.), *The Indo-Aryans of Ancient South Asia*, Berlin. 293–306.
Sax, William (2002), *Dancing the Self*, New York.
Scheuer, Jacques (1982), *Śiva Dans le Mahābhārata*, Paris.
Schlingloff, Dieter (1969), "The Oldest Extant Parvan List of the Māhabhārata," *Journal of the American Oriental Society* 89.2: 334–338.
Seaford, Richard (2004), *Money and the Early Greek Mind*, Cambridge.

Selvanayagam, Israel (1992–93), "Aśoka and Arjuna as Counterfigures Standing on the Field of Dharma," *History Of Religions* 32: 59–75.
Sen, Amartya (2009), *The Idea of Justice*, Delhi.
von Simson, Georg (1968), "The Mythic Origin of Droṇa and Karṇa," *Journal of the Bihar Research Society* 54: 40–44.
Skjærvø, Prods Oktor (1998), "Eastern Iranian Epic Traditions I: Siyāvaś and Kunāla," in: *Mír Curad, Studies in Honour of Calvert Watkins*, ed. Jay Jasanoff, H. Craig Melchert, and Lisi Olivier, Innsbruck, 645–658.
——— (2000), "Eastern Iranian Epic Traditions III: Zarathustra and Diomedes. An Indo-European Epic Warrior Type," *Bulletin of the Asia Institute* 11: 175–182.
Smith, J. D. (1987), "Formulaic Language in the Epics of India." in: *The Heroic Process: Form, Function, and Fantasy in Folk Epic*, ed. Bo Almqvist, Séamas Ó Catháin, and Pádraig Héalai, Dublin, 591–611.
—— (1991), *The Epic of Pābūjī*, Cambridge.
Smith, M. C. (1975), "The Mahābhārata's Core," *Journal of the American Oriental Society* 95.3: 479–482.
—— (1992), *The Warrior Code of India's Sacred Song*, New York.
Snodgrass, Anthony (1998), *Homer and the Artists*, Cambridge.
Snodgrass, Jeffrey G. (2006), *Casting Kings*, New York.
Sörensen, S. (1904), *An Index to the Names in the Mahābhārata*, repr. 1978, Delhi.
Squarcini, Federico, ed. (2005), *Boundaries, Dynamics, and Construction of Traditions in South Asia*, Florence.
Sukthankar, Vishnu S. (1944), *Critical Studies in the Mahābhārata*, Bombay.
—— (1959), *Mahābhārata*, 19 vols., Poona.
Sullivan, Bruce (1990), *Kṛṣṇa Dvaipāyana Vyāsa and the Mahābhārata*, Leiden.
Sutton, Nick (1997), "Aśoka and Yudhiṣṭhira," *Religion* 27.4: 333–341.
Tharoor, Shashi (1989), *The Great Indian Novel*, New Delhi.
Tharoor, Shashi and Susan S. Bean (2006), *Epic India: M. F. Husain's Mahabharata Project*, Salem, Mass.
Vansina, J. (1985), *Oral Tradition as History*, Madison.
Vassilkov, Yaroslav (1995), "The Mahābhārata's Typological Definition Considered," *Indo-Iranian Journal* 38: 249–256.
de Vries, J. (1963), *Heroic Song and Heroic Legend*, trans. B. J. Timmer, Oxford.
Watkins, Calvert, ed. (1985), *The American Heritage Dictionary of Indo-European Roots*, Boston.
—— (1995), *How to Kill a Dragon. Aspects of Indo-European Poetics*, Oxford.
—— (2002), "Pindar's Rigveda," *Journal of the American Oriental Society* 122: 432–434.
West, M. L. (2007), *Indo-European Poetry and Myth*, Oxford.
Wiser, William Henricks (1936), *The Hindu Jajmani System*, Lucknow.

Index

CPSIA information can be obtained at www.ICGtesting.com
Printed in the USA
BVOW032357031211

277245BV00007B/42/P

9 780674 062467